INSTANT
AUSSIE

Australia in a Nutshell

JASON K. FOSTER

First published in 2015 by New Holland Publishers Pty Ltd
London • Sydney • Auckland

The Chandlery Unit 009 50 Westminster Bridge Road London SE1 7QY United Kingdom
1/66 Gibbes Street Chatswood NSW 2067 Australia
5/39 Woodside Ave Northcote, Auckland 0627 New Zealand

www.newhollandpublishers.com

A record of this book is held at the British Library and the National Library of Australia.

ISBN 9781742577425

Managing Director: Fiona Schultz
Publisher: Alan Whiticker
Project Editor: Holly Willsher
Designer: Peter Guo
Production Director: Olga Dementiev
Printer: Toppan Leefung Printing Limited

10 9 8 7 6 5 4 3 2 1

Keep up with New Holland Publishers on Facebook
www.facebook.com/NewHollandPublishers

Contents

Introduction

The current Prime Minister of Australia, Tony Abbott, in his New Year's Eve speech to the nation said, 'living in Australia is like winning the lottery.' And considering we refer to ourselves as the 'Lucky Country', he's probably right.

Aussies, while we all agree our country is the greatest, have different reasons for thinking so. Some believe it is our education system that makes us tops, others believe it is the equal opportunities and rights for men and for women or the freedom we have to say whatever we want and think whatever we like. Add into this: barbeques, multiculturalism, our mates and last, but by no means least, our beautiful landscape and climate.

No matter which of the above reason an Aussie favours, there is one thing we all agree on: Australia is God's country.

According to the Australian Trade Commission (*www.austrade.gov.au*) a record 6.3 million short-term visitors came to Australia for the year ending June 2013.

New Zealand, unsurprisingly, accounts for the greatest source of short-term arrivals, with more than a million Kiwis making the quick hop across the Tasman Sea every year. Following the Kiwis are the Brits and the Americans (again, no surprise, as they are our two biggest allies and two large, English speaking countries). The number of American visitors in 2013 was actually the highest it has been since the Sydney 2000 Olympics. The biggest growth in tourists is the Chinese (with 685,000 arrivals in 2013), making up 10.9 per cent of Australia's total short-term tourists.

Yes, we're the country everyone wants to visit and why wouldn't they? We are the world's largest island in the world (people often say Greenland, but we're bigger) and the only island to call itself a continent. We have everything ranging from the world's best beaches, to rainforest, to ski fields to the renowned red dust of the Outback.

Our former Prime Minister, Paul Keating, once referred to Australia as, 'the arse end of the world.' Geographically, depending on your point of view, this may be true but we are a tourist and immigration Mecca, but what exactly makes that so? What makes hundreds of thousands of people want to come here on a working visa? What makes hundreds of thousands more want to permanently move to the arse end of the world?

Simple…

According to the Organisation for Economic Co-operation and Development (OECD) Better Life Index, 2014, (*www.oced.org*) we are ranked number 1 for the most desirable places to live in the world. This is based on the fact that:

- We have a long life-expectancy (82.10 years);
- We are involved in our government (voting is compulsory);
- We have a high level of life satisfaction;
- We have a good work-life balance (Australians were some of the first to pioneer the push for an 8 hour day);
- We have a good average income ($75, 000 per annum), good housing (70% of people own or are paying off their own homes), and good jobs (unemployment is 6.6%, but that is the highest it has been in years!).

Aussies are a laid-back, easy-going people. We devote ourselves to our work and we work hard to get what we want. We are, however, masters at the art of relaxation and, when we're not working, we're surfing, swimming or playing some kind of sport (which, come to think of it, makes it difficult to understand why we are starting to become one of the fattest countries in the world).

Aussies have a distinct sense of humour, which sometimes other people don't get. We have a form of English unlike anything else and we have an accent like no other – one which no one else in the world seems to be able to master or imitate. Even the quintessential Australia phrase, 'g'day,' seems to be too much of a stretch.

Speaking of the rest of the world, Aussies love to travel, but in the immortal words of the late, great Peter Allen – 'We still call Australia home.'

We love our cricket and even the most reluctant fan can be found sitting down in front of the telly on Boxing Day to watch the Test match. We love nothing better than thrashing the Poms (the English) in the Ashes but also, well, pretty much anything else we can.

We love our footy but we are fiercely competitive amongst ourselves about which type of the three traditional types of football: soccer, rugby union, rugby league is the best.

We dearly love our own creation, Australian Rules.

We also have fierce sporting rivalries with New Zealand, mostly when it comes to rugby, but we consider New Zealand out little brother so we take great joy when New Zealand beats anyone else apart from us (although, apparently, New Zealanders don't always share this camaraderie!). And when we do have high achievers coming from our little bro, New Zealand, we just claim them as our own – such as Russell Crowe and Crowded House.

We are proud of who we are. We are proud of our country. However, to best explain the land of Australia and how we feel about it, there is no more appropriate way than a verse from one of our most renowned poems from one of our best poets.

I Love a Sunburnt Country
by Dorothy Mackellar
(Second Verse)

I love a sunburnt country,
A land of sweeping plains,
Of ragged mountain ranges,
Of droughts and flooding rains.
I love her far horizons,
I love her jewel-sea,
Her beauty and her terror -
The wide brown land for me!

Australia. A big, open, yet empty, country unlike anywhere else in the world...

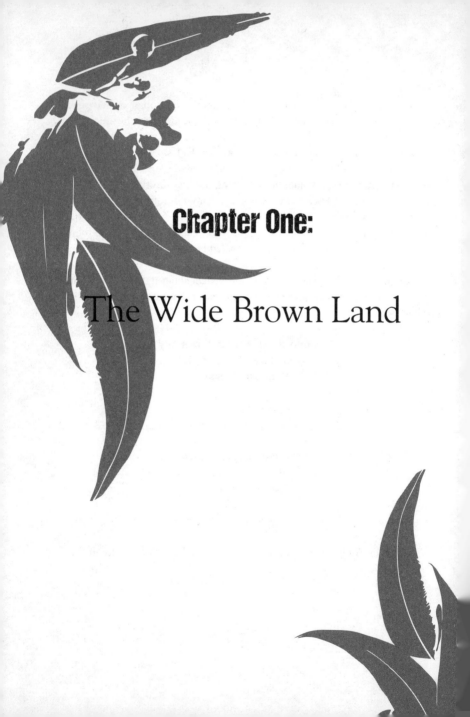

Chapter One:

The Wide Brown Land

Just How Big is Australia?

Australia has six states: New South Wales (NSW), Queensland (QLD), Victoria (VIC), Tasmania (TAS), South Australia (SA) and Western Australia (WA) and two territories: The Australian Capital Territory (ACT) and the Northern Territory (NT).

Australia makes up 5.2 per cent of the world's total land surface, and yet we only make up 0.003 per cent of the world's population. Australia is the world's the sixth largest country behind Russia, Canada, the United States, China and Brazil.

Australians know we have a big country, but sometimes we don't even realise how big our country really is! Australia is:

- 14 times larger than France.
- 20 times bigger than Japan.
- 26 times larger than Italy.
- 28 times bigger than New Zealand.
- 32 times bigger than the United Kingdom.
- 186 times larger than Switzerland.
- 12000 times bigger than Singapore.
- 4 million times bigger than Monaco.
- 17 million times bigger than the Vatican City.

Some further comparisons may help to make more sense of it. Australia is:

- About the same size of the mainland 48 states of America.
- Slightly bigger than the whole continent of Europe.
- Bigger than all of Southeast Asia.

And some more facts about the size of Australia:

- The Australian mainland's northernmost point is the tip of Cape York Peninsula, QLD, (approx. 11 degrees south).
- The Australian mainland's southernmost point is South Point, Wilson's Promontory, VIC, (39 degrees south).

- The Australian mainland's westernmost point is Steep Point, WA, (113 degrees east). The Australian mainland's easternmost point is Cape Byron, NSW, (approx. 139 degrees east).

As you can see from the above statistics mainland Australia measures over 28 degrees of latitude and spans 26 degrees of longitude.

Australia's actual geographic borders extend further:

- Australia's actual northernmost point is Bramble Cay, in the Torres Strait Islands, QLD (approx. 9 degrees south).
- Australia's actual southernmost point is the Bishop and Clerk Islets, (approx. 55 degrees south).
- Australia's actual easternmost point is Steel's Point, Norfolk Island, (approx. 168 degrees east).
- Australia's actual westernmost point is the Heard and McDonald Islands, (approx. 73 degrees east).

Australia has a range of mountains running the length of the east coast from Victoria to Queensland, called The Great Dividing Range. Within this range, in an area known as The Snowy Mountains, you will find Australia's highest mountain, Mount Kosciusko (2228 metres/ 7310 feet above sea level) or, if you include the outer territories, Australia's highest peak is Mawson Peak on the Heard and McDonald Islands (2745 metres/ 9006 feet above sea level). In the central parts of Australia there is a semi-dry salt lake, Lake Eyre, which is Australia's lowest point at 15 metres below sea level.

Therefore, in actuality, Australia covers 46 degrees of latitude and 95 degrees of longitude!

Australia has over 10000 beaches and is bordered by two great oceans, the Indian Ocean in the west and the Pacific Ocean in the east. We also have the Tasman Sea separating us from New Zealand, the Southern Sea separating us from Antarctica and the Arafura Sea separating us from East Timor and Indonesia.

Mainland Australia crosses three time zones which can be confusing for the foreign visitor because Western Australia is three hours behind New South Wales while South Australia and the Northern Territory are only half an hour behind, but then this all changes in the summertime with Daylight Savings which means that New South Wales, Victoria, South Australia put their clocks forward an hour. Queensland, Western Australia and the Northern Territory don't which means that Australia then has several different times zones.

If you're confused, don't worry this confuses us too!

How Far Down Under is 'Down Under'?

Most people around the world, due mostly in part to the worldwide success of Men at Work's song, *Down Under*, refer to Australia as the land 'down under'. Even the most geographically challenged American still knows that Australia is a long way from anywhere but if the European explorers could spend six months or more on a boat to get here, then anyone can!

Let's take a look…

Australia is (approximately):

- 7000 kilometres from the South Pole.
- 12000 kilometres from Disneyland.
- 13500 kilometres from Machu Picchu.
- 14000 kilometres from the North Pole.
- 14500 kilometres from The Pyramids.
- 16806 kilometres from Timbuktu.
- 17000 kilometres from the Eiffel Tower.
- And, as for the rest of the world…

How Long Does It Take To Get Here?

City of Origin	Distance	Flight Time (Minimum – Bear in mind it might take much, much longer…)
Amsterdam	16639 km/ 10339 miles	21 hours
Athens	15326 km/ 9523 miles	20 hours
Auckland	2159 km/ 1342 miles	3 hours
Bangkok	7524 km/ 4675 miles	10 hours
Beijing	8923 km/ 5545 miles	12 hours
Berlin	16090 km/ 9998 miles	21 hours
Buenos Aires	11822 km/ 7346 miles	17 hours
Delhi	10419 km/ 6474 miles	13 hours
Dublin	17211 km/ 10694 miles	22 hours
Dubai	12048 km/ 7486 miles	15 hours
Jakarta	5500 km/ 3417 miles	7 hours
Johannesburg	11058 km/ 6871 miles	14 hours
London	16991 km/ 10558 miles	22 hours
Madrid	17688 km/ 10991 miles	23 hours
Mexico City	12973 km/ 8061 miles	17 hours
Paris	16960 km/ 10538 miles	21 hours
Moscow	14486 km/ 9001 miles	19 hours
Singapore	6305 km/ 3918 miles	8 hours
Tokyo	7793 km/ 4842 miles	10 hours
Vancouver	12482 km/ 7756 miles	16 hours

Getting Around Down Under: Domestic Flying Times and Driving in Australia

The unwary traveller might think that after spending almost a full day in transit that the flight pain would end there but they would be mistaken.

Flying time and distance in kilometres from Sydney to other major cities in Australia...

Location	Adelaide	Alice Springs	Brisbane	Cairns	Canberra	Darwin	Melbourne	Perth
Distance (km)	1165	2029	728	1957	240	3,151	706	3274
Distance (miles)	724	1261	453	1216	149	1958	440	2034
Time	1 hour 57 mins	3 hours	1 hour 25 mins	3 hours	48 mins	4 hours 40 mins	1 hour 20 mins	4 hours 10 mins

No problem, I hear you say, I will just hire a car. Except...it takes about three days to drive across one of the largest deserts in the world, to get from Sydney to Perth.

Driving Distances (in Kilometres) Between Major Australian Cities

Location	Adel	Alice Springs	Bris	Cairns	Canberra	Darwin	Melb	Perth	Syd
Adel	X	1533	2044	3143	1204	3042	728	2725	1427
Alice	1533	X	3100	2500	2680	1489	2270	3630	2850
Bris	2044	3100	X	1718	1268	3415	1669	4384	1010
Cairns	3143	2500	1718	X	2922	3100	3387	5954	2730
Canberra	1204	2680	1268	2922	X	3917	647	3911	288
Darwin	3042	1489	3415	3100	3917	X	4045	4250	3991
Melb	728	2270	1669	3387	647	4045	X	3430	963
Perth	2725	3630	4384	5954	3911	4250	3430	X	4110
Sydney	1427	2850	1010	2730	288	3991	963	4110	X

Time Taken By Road in Driving Hours

Location	Adel	Alice Springs	Bris	Cairns	Canberra	Darwin	Melb	Perth	Syd
Adel	X	16	23	38	16	24	9	30	14
Alice	16	X	37	30	32	18	24	40	32
Bris	23	37	X	21	16	44	19	53	11
Cairns	38	30	21	X	35	37	40	75	32
Canberra	16	32	16	35	X	43	7	43	3
Darwin	24	18	44	37	43	X	55	49	43
Melb	9	24	19	40	7	55	X	39	9
Perth	30	40	53	75	43	49	39	X	9
Sydney	15	32	11	32	3	43	9	44	X

Local Knowledge: A Few Tips on Driving in Australia

Due to our tremendous size, long distance travel is second nature to Aussies. Any Aussie you speak to will have childhood memories of sitting in the car for a ten-hour, or more, drive (getting bored, and pinching, punching or whacking your sister and pretending you didn't do anything, hours of 'I-Spy' and even more hours of asking your parents, 'are we there yet?') to go and see family members in Melbourne or Queensland, or thinking nothing of driving six hours to go on a camping holiday.

If you do choose to drive in Australian cities be prepared, be very prepared! Driving in Australia brings a whole range of potentialities for death or injury. So, here are a few things you need to know:

- *Left or Right?* - Unlike most of the world, except maybe England and New Zealand or other Commonwealth countries, we drive on the left.
- *Seat Belts* - It is required by law that all passengers and the driver wear a seatbelt, if a passenger is not wearing a seatbelt it is the driver's responsibility. Additionally, any child under the age of 7 must be secured in an approved child restraint capsule.
- *Drink Driving* - In Australia is a crime and you have a high chance of having to undertake a Random Breath Test (RBT) which can be performed by any police officer at any time but they are usually conducted at designated roadside areas. The legal alcohol limit to be driving is 0.05 (equivalent to one standard drink per hour). Driving over the legal alcohol limit incurs very serious penalties, including large fines and, in extreme cases, jail terms.
- *Road Trains* – These are large, multi-trailer transport trucks that can measure up to 53.5 metres long (176 feet) and are a common sight on Outback highways. The best advice when coming across a Road Train is to pull over as far as you can to the opposite side of the road or stop to completely avoid them. When overtaking a Road Train allow 1.5 kilometres (0.8 miles) of clear road and be careful of the dust clouds!
- *Driver Fatigue* – Along with alcohol and speeding, driver fatigue is one of the leading causes of road fatalities in Australia. Across Australia there

are 'Driver Revivers' where motorists can have a free cup of coffee and a 'bikkie' (biscuit) or a Kit Kat (chocolate). Experts recommend a break from driving every two hours.

- *Speed* – Across most Australian states the maximum speed limit on highways is between 100 and 110 kph (approximately 60–65 mph). However, in some parts of the Northern Territory and other parts of the Outback you may see a black circle with a black line through it, which means there is no speed limit. Local speed limits in towns and cities range between 50 and 80 kph (30–45mph). Be particularly careful around school times (8–9:30am/ 2:30–4pm) as the limit around schools drops to 40 kph (approx. 22–25 mph). Police operate both mobile and static speed cameras. And, if you're thinking to yourself, never mind I come from another country, the Australian police will send a fine to your home address.

- *Outback Driving* – Many Australian roads are unsealed but, given our vast size, many of our sealed roads are also a long way from anywhere. Your best bet is to get as much detail as you can from locals about driving conditions. Also, the Top End (northern parts of the Northern Territory/ Queensland and Western Australia) is situated in the tropics. This means they only have two seasons, wet and dry (dry season – March to November, wet season – December to February). During the wet season driving conditions can change in an instant and, thus, become much more dangerous with flooded rivers or muddy roads.

- If you intend on driving in the Outback it is a good idea to let local authorities know exactly where you plan to go because, if you do break down, you can be easily located. If you break down in the bush DO NOT LEAVE YOUR CAR! With temperatures often reaching above 45 degrees you won't last very long. People who stay with their cars are the ones most likely to survive!

- *Aboriginal Land* – Many parts of Australia are owned by Aboriginal people (for example, Arnhem Land in the Northern Territory) and, if you intend to enter Aboriginal lands you will need to obtain permission to do so.

Gaining a permit is different from state to state and it can take some time to get the necessary permits.

- *Wildlife* – Australia's wildlife can be a huge danger to the driver. Many Australian animals are attracted to car headlights or try to cross the road at night. Two of the most dangerous animals are the red kangaroo and farmer's cattle. Needless to say, if a big animal such as this hits your car you will be in for some serious damage. Hitting large animals is so common that many Australian cars will have bull bars (extra steel protection) fitted to the front of their car.

The Natural Wonders of Australia

Australians, to be honest, sometimes take our fantastic natural wonders for granted, but we are truly blessed with what we have. While you could drive, or sail, anywhere in Australia and see awe-inspiring landscapes there are some absolute must-sees.

1. The Great Barrier Reef

Named by Captain James Cook, because when he encountered the reef it formed a 'barrier', the reef is the world's largest. At over 3000 kilometres long, the Great Barrier Reef is visible from space. The Great Barrier Reef has 400 types of coral and 1500 species of fish as well as sharks, rays, moray eels, and jellyfish.

The Barrier Reef is one of the best places (if not the best place) to snorkel and scuba dive but it is under severe environmental threat. There are two major threats to the Great Barrier Reef:

- *The Crown of Thorns Starfish*: Named so because it looks like the crown of thorns Jesus wore as he carried his cross. This nasty creature, according to the Great Barrier Reef Marine Authority, has caused, on its own, the coral cover of the reef to decline by almost 50 per cent over the last 30 years. There are control methods in place but authorities are still to find a lasting solution.
- *Climate Change*: The most significant way that climate change could affect the reef is in the bleaching of the coral. Coral polyps require the water to

be a certain temperature and the rising temperatures kill (or bleach) the coral. Climate change can also affect the reef through increased and more severe weather events, which in turn, will increase acidification of the ocean and damage the reef through rising sea levels.

Best experienced: By taking a boat and snorkelling or scuba diving.

2. Uluru/ Kata Tjuta

The great, red monolith of a rock is almost in the dead centre of the country and the ultimate symbol of the Australian Outback. Many people know Uluru as Ayer's Rock (because explorer William Gosse discovered it in 1873 and named it after the then Chief Secretary of South Australia, Sir Henry Ayers) and many people still make the mistake of calling it this to this day. However, as part of the Land Rights movement to give back part of the country to the Aboriginal people the rock was returned to its traditional owners and the name was changed to its traditional name, Uluru.

- Uluru is situated in the Uluru-Kata Tjuta National Park. It is 348 metres high and has a circumference of 9.4 kilometres. It is a sacred site to the Indigenous Anangu people and, if you were thinking about climbing it, think about the following statement from the Anangu: 'The climb is not prohibited, but we ask you to respect our law and culture by not climbing Uluru. We have a responsibility to teach and safeguard visitors to our land. The climb can be dangerous. Too many people have died while attempting to climb Uluru. Many others have been injured while climbing. We feel great sadness when a person dies or is hurt on our land. We worry about you and we worry about your family. Our traditional law teaches us the proper way to behave.' (*www.parksaustralia.gov.au*)

Best experienced: At sunrise or sunset to experience the bright reds and purples of the Outback.

Kata Tjuta

Kata Tjuta (sometimes referred to as the Olgas) is near to Uluru. They are a large, domed rock formation. There are 36 'domes' and Kata Tjuta covers almost 22 square kilometres. Composed of similar type rocks to Uluru walking through Kata Tjuta is just as amazing as seeing the big rock.

3. Shark Bay/ Monkey Mia

Shark Bay, approximately 800 kilometres north of Perth, has great historical significance as the site where the Dutch explorer, Dirk Hartog, landed in 1616. However, for the modern visitor to Australia the white sand dunes and kilometres of beautiful coastline, as well as many dugongs (up to 10000) and dolphins, make it the perfect destination.

Monkey Mia

Ask any Australian about Monkey Mia and the first word they will say to you is, 'dolphins.'

Thousands of tourists, for almost 40 years, have been flocking to Monkey Mia to see the bottlenose dolphins that come in for a daily feed. The Department of Environment and Conservation have, quite rightly, imposed strict feeding limits but all tourists will get to both feed and frolic with the dolphins without having to jump in for a swim with them.

The dolphins are only fed on their first three visits, which can occur between morning and midday.

Best experienced: Summers and early in the morning.

4. The Twelve Apostles

The Twelve Apostles are huge limestone towers just off the southern coast of Victoria and part of the Port Campbell National Park. Some of the limestone stacks can reach up to 45 metres high and the Apostles provide a view into Australia's ancient, ancient history. In 2012, however, time's endless march continued and wind and water erosion, unfortunately, led to some of the columns collapsing so, the Twelve Apostles, are now down to 8. This does not make them any less stunning though!

Best experienced: Whilst taking a road trip along one of Australia's best drives, the Great Ocean Road.

5. Fraser Island

World Heritage listed and the world's largest sand island, Fraser Island (or K'gari/ paradise to the Indigenous people) is 123 kilometres long and 22 kilometres wide. A popular destination for four-wheel drivers who head up and down the pristine white beaches and for fisherman also who cast their lines into the crystal clear Pacific Ocean. Fraser Island also has more than 100 freshwater lakes and tall sand dunes. The island is home to an array of wildlife including dugongs and sea turtles, however the most famous animal on the island is the dingo. Fraser Island is the home of the last pure dingoes in Australia as many of the dingoes in other parts of Australia have been interbred with introduced dogs. Make sure you don't feed the dingoes, though, as they have been known to attack people.

Best experienced: Any time of the year!

6. Kakadu National Park

Another World Heritage listed part of Australia is Kakadu, probably the most famous National Park in our country. Kakadu is in the Northern Territory and covers almost 20, 000 square kilometres. It is 240 kilometres from the state capital, Darwin, and is the traditional lands of the Bininj/ Mungguy people. Kakadu attracts hundreds of thousands of visitors from abroad and from home every year. The park's main attraction is, of course, the saltwater crocodiles but there is also an array of birds and other wildlife as well as elements of Aboriginal culture such as rock art and paintings.

Controversially, Kakadu has the Ranger Uranium Mine smack bang in the middle of it.

Best experienced: Any time of the year but depending on what you want to see, choose carefully between the wet and dry season.

7. The Blue Mountains

The Blue Mountains are part of the Great Dividing Range and are about two hours' drive out of Sydney. Most famed for the large sandstone rock formations known as the Three Sisters, the Blue Mountains is a series of sandstone plateaus and ridgelines. The name 'blue' mountains, comes from the evaporation of the eucalyptus oil that give the mountains a bluish tinge. The mountains are the traditional lands of two Aboriginal nations, the Darug people in the lower mountains and the Gundungarra people in the upper mountains.

The Blue Mountains are rich in flora and fauna such as kangaroos and koalas and it is also home to the Wollemi Pine, one of the oldest and rarest trees in the world.

Best Experienced: All year round, but winter in the mountains is magical.

Local Knowledge: The Story of the Three Sisters
One version anyway…

Back in dreamtime, there were three sisters, Meenhi, Wimlah and Gunnedoo. Their father was the tribe's witch doctor and his name was Tyawan.

The sisters, their father and their tribe lived a happy life but for the one thing they feared the most, the Bunyip. The Bunyip lived in a deep hole and very few people ever crossed his path.

Whenever Tyawan had no choice but to venture past the hole in search of food he would tell his daughters to wait behind on the cliff and to conceal themselves behind a large rocky wall.

One day, Tyawan, happy his daughters were safe, waved goodbye to them and headed down the steep cliff face and into the valley below.

Just as their father disappeared into the rainforest a large centipede crawled across the cliff in front of Meenhi. Frightened and scared, Meenhi picked up a huge rock and threw it at the centipede. The stone, missed the centipede, and continued on, tumbling and rolling its way down the cliffs and into the valley.

The crash and echo of the stone as it bounced off the cliffs woke the Bunyip. Angry to have his sleep disturbed he started bashing and crashing his way out of his hole.

High above, the cliff face on which the girls stood began to shake. Parts of the cliff began to break away and then the rocky wall, which the girls were hiding behind, began to crumble.

Meenhi, Wimlah and Gunnedoo were left stranded on a thin ledge at the top of the cliff. All the birds, animals and even the fairies stopped still as the

Bunyip emerged. He looked around to see who had woken him and, when he lifted his head skywards, he saw the terrified girls, huddled together and hoping he would not see them.

Their hopes were dashed as, ever so slowly; the Bunyip began to climb the cliffs. Just at this moment, Tyawan returned and, seeing the Bunyip edging closer and closer to his beloved daughters, he hurriedly used his magic bone and turned the girls to stone.

His girls were safe but when the Bunyip saw what Tyawan had done he was furious and he began to chase him. Tyawan ran and ran through the tracks of the rainforest but the Bunyip was coming closer and closer. In order to escape the Bunyip, Tyawan had to turn himself into a magnificent Lyrebird but, in doing so, he dropped his magic bone.

The Bunyip stopped in his tracks and, realising he had lost his prey, returned to his hole. Tyawan hid in the ferns until he was sure the Bunyip was gone. When he was certain he was safe he began to search for his magic bone, but it was nowhere to be found.

Tyawan, the Lyrebird, has been searching for this magic bone ever since. His daughters are still rocks in formation, standing way above the valley waiting for the day that their father finds his magic bone and he can turn them back.

When you visit The Three Sisters, make sure you listen carefully. You may just hear the sounds of the Lyrebird on the wind, Tyawan still questing for his magic bone.

For more information on the story of The Three Sisters and the Blue Mountains visit, *www.bluemountainsaustralia.com*

8. Port Arthur and Sarah Island

For any foreign visitor interested in understanding and learning more about Australia's colonial history, Port Arthur and Sarah Island are a must see. Port Arthur is located approximately 100 kilometres from Hobart and is actually an open-air museum. The UNESCO World Heritage List describes Port Arthur as, 'the best surviving examples of large-scale convict transportation of European powers through the presence and labour of convicts.'

Port Arthur was one of the harshest penal settlements in Australia, meant for the hardest of British criminals and convicts who had committed offences after their transportation to Australia as well as persons who were considered unruly or rebellious. Hence, the security and discipline at Port Arthur were rather strict.

Sarah Island housed the Macquarie Harbour Penal Settlement and was only in operation for 11 years, from 1822 to 1833. If convicts feared Port Arthur, then they absolutely dreaded Sarah Island. Macquarie Harbour has rough seas and is isolated, even for Tasmanian standards. The worst of the worst convicts were sent here as well as persistent escape artists.

Best experienced: In the spring and summer time as the seas, and weather, can be quite treacherous during the winter months.

9. Cradle Mountain

Tasmania has many natural gems but Cradle Mountain is something else again. Cradle Mountain is in the Cradle Mountain-Lake St Clair National Park. It sits about 1550 metres above sea level. Cradle Mountain is a dolomite formation and is famed for its beautiful alpine flora. Cradle Mountain is also an excellent place to see wombats, echidnas and, of course, Tassie Devils.

Cradle Mountain (and Dove Lake) is breathtaking just to view but the area is also an outstanding area for hiking. The trails in the area have huts for overnight hikers, however it is not recommended to undertake overnight hikes without proper supplies and informing the authorities of your plans.

Best experienced: During spring and summer while hiking is possible.

10. The Daintree Rainforest

The Daintree Rainforest is a tropical rainforest in the far north of Queensland. It measures around 12000 square kilometres and is, consequently, the largest tropical rainforest in Australia.

The Daintree is, mostly, a national park and the Australian and Queensland governments are endeavouring to make the park bigger by buying nearby private property and as they rightly should. The rainforest is home to 3 per cent of Australia's frog, reptile and marsupial species, 90 per cent of bat and butterfly species and 7 per cent of bird species.

The landscape covers everything from mountain ranges, stunning streams, massive gorges and dense rainforest. To see what Australia was like millions of years ago, one cannot miss out on a trip to the Daintree.

Best experienced: All year round, but preferably in the dry season to make moving through the forest much easier.

Everything in Australia is Big!

Dotted across our country there are more than 150 'big' things in Australia.

The big things in Australia make the perfect excuse for a road trip or, if you are driving around the country, they make a perfect excuse to stop for a cuppa. There are too many to list (see, *www.australianpictorials.com/big_things*) but here are the most famous ones...

New South Wales

The Big Banana

Coffs Harbour has the perfect climate for bananas so most farmers around the area grow them. Consequently, Coffs Harbour has a Big Banana. It is one of the most famous icons of the town and was the first big thing in New South Wales, being more than 40 years old.

The Big Cheese

Located on the south coast, Bodalla is not only a town; it is one of our most famous cheese brands. The region is renowned for the quality of their cheeses; therefore Bodalla has the Big Cheese.

The Big Golden Guitar

The Tamworth Country Music Festival is the biggest in the country and to be awarded a Golden Guitar is one of the highest honours an Australian country artist can receive. Given Tamworth's place as the country music capital of Australia it only makes sense to have a big guitar.

The Big Merino

Goulburn, in the Southern Highlands, is sheep country. Australia, as the saying goes, became wealthy off 'the sheep's back.' So, why not celebrate that with a giant sheep!

The Big Prawn

Ballina, on the northern coast, has prawn fishing as one of its main industries. Some of the best prawns in the country are to be eaten here, but not the Big Prawn!

Northern Territory

The Big Stubby

Located in Larrimah, the Big Stubby is about 428 kilometres southeast of Darwin. The town had its heyday in the Second World War when it was used as an Australian Army base. Now, the town's population is only 11 and the Big Stubby sits outside the local pub.

Queensland

The Big Macadamia Nut

Nambour, on the Sunshine Coast, is the home to the Big Macadamia Nut. The macadamia nut is one of the only forms of bush tucker (traditional Indigenous foods) that is produced at a commercial level. You can try some of these fantastic nuts and there is even a 'Nut Mobile' to have a ride on.

The Big Mango

Near the heartland of the mango growing region of Queensland the town of Bowen has the Big Mango. The most interesting thing about the Big Mango, in recent times, was that it was stolen, apparently as part of a publicity stunt to promote a new dish for Nando's chicken!

The Big Pineapple

Also in Nambour, the Big Pineapple is a heritage-listed 'building'. One of the main crops out of Queensland is the pineapple and the climate in the region is perfect for growing them. The Big Pineapple also has a railway, which takes tourists on a ride around the nearby pineapple plantations.

South Australia

The Big Scotsman

Due to the fact that New South Wales and Queensland have most of the 150 big things, credit for the first big thing often goes to the Big Banana, except the distinction of the first 'big' thing in Australia should actually go to the Big Scotsman. Located in the town of Medindie, the Big Scotsman was built in 1963 as a promotional tool for Scotty's Motel.

The Big Galah

The Big Galah is at Kimba, which is exactly half way across Australia. Kimba is on the Eyre Highway, a long stretch of road across the Nullarbor Plain. As such, the café at the Big Galah makes a good place to take a break.

The Big Kangaroo

A 5 metre high kangaroo at Bordertown (on the border between South Australia and Western Australia). The roo now holds a can of soft drink in its left paw but it is thought that this can used to be a can of beer and, given Australia's love of a beer, this seems likely!

The Big Lobster

Affectionately known as 'Larry' to the locals of Kingston, the lobster is 17 metres tall, thus making it one of the most impressive big things in Australia.

The best part about visiting Larry is that Kingston is renowned for big lobsters, so it is hard to imagine a tastier truck stop.

Tasmania

The Big Platypus

Platypi can be hard to spot in the wild, even for the keenest-eyed Aussie. If you want to see a platypus in its natural habitat it might be worth taking a trip to the Big Platypus in Latrobe. Located at the Platypus Interpretation Centre (and, no, this does not mean they speak Platypus). It does mean that the Centre runs two-hour tours through the Warrawee Forest so that the visitor can see one of our strangest animals in its natural environment.

The Big Tasmanian Devil

The Big Tassie Devil lives at Trowunna Wildlife Park at Mole Creek. While you can see the big Devil out the front of the park, the park itself is quite small and this means you will be able to get very up-close and personal with a real Devil!

Victoria

The Big Milkshake

Warrnambool is one of Australia's leading dairy areas and consequently do, debatably, the best milkshakes in the country. The Big Milkshake is around 8 metres tall and sits outside Cheese World.

The Big Ned Kelly

The name of the town Glenrowan is synonymous with the bushranger, Ned Kelly, and, more specifically his final shootout with Victorian police. Glenrowan not only has the 7 metre high statue of Kelly himself but also anything else about Ned Kelly you could possibly think of!

The Big Strawberry

If you're a strawberry lover you definitely need to pay a visit to the Big Strawberry at Koonoomoo in north-western Victoria. The best part about the Big Strawberry is that you get to pick your own and then try every imaginable strawberry treat in the nearby café.

Western Australia

The Big Magic Mushroom

Without doubt the strangest and oddest choice of a big thing to have in a town is the Big Magic Mushroom. Balingup is a little over 200 km south of Perth and, apparently, is renowned for the amount of magic mushrooms growing in the nearby forests. This has attracted a lot of people seeking an 'alternative' lifestyle but, police from the nearby town of Donnybrook will surely have something to say about this!

World's Tallest Bin

Mystery surrounds the origins of the World's Tallest Bin in the gold mining town of Kalgoorlie but, apparently, the 8 metre high bin was put in place as part of the Tidy Town competition (something which Australian country towns take very seriously) and the residents just never bothered to take it down.

Local Knowledge: Place names you won't find on the map

There are a lot of places in Australia that no tourist will find on any map, no matter how hard they look.

Across the Ditch	The 'Ditch' is the stretch of water between Australia and New Zealand.
Apple Isle	Tasmania – due to the large numbers of Apples grown on the island.
The Antipodes	Antipodes being Latin for south. The Antipodes encompass Australia, South Africa and New Zealand and any of those citizens consider themselves 'Antipodeans'.
The Back of Beyond	Any place away from the main cities.
The Back of Bourke	While Bourke is a town in the far west of New South Wales, the Back of Bourke is used to refer to anywhere way out in the Outback.
Beyond the Black Stump	A long way from anywhere.
Big Smoke	One of the major cities, usually Sydney, Melbourne or Brisbane.
The Boondocks/ The Boonies	A far off area – colloquialism for the countryside.
Brissie	Queensland's capital, Brisbane.
Brisvegas	Queensland's capital, Brisbane.
Bullamakanka	A mythical place in the middle of nowhere.
The City of Churches	Adelaide – due to the city's numerous churches.
The City of Lights	Perth.
The Cross	Short for King's Cross – the red light district of Sydney.
Down Under	A colloquialism for either Australia or New Zealand and, sometimes, both.
Harbour City	Sydney.

Mulga	The Bush.
Never Never	Another name for a far off place.
North Island	How Tasmanians refer to the mainland.
Paris on the Yarra	Melbourne.
Scrub	Bush or Outback.
The Alice	Alice Springs, a town in central Australia.
The 'G'	The Melbourne Cricket Ground or MCG.
The Gabba	The Woolloongabba Cricket Ground in Brisbane.
The Golden Mile	The main street of King's Cross in Sydney/ Kalgoorlie, Western Australia's, main street.
The Gong	Wollongong, a city an hour's drive south of Sydney.
The Emerald City	Sydney.
The Steel City	Newcastle.
The Top End	Anywhere north of the Tropic of Capricorn but generally used to refer to the top part of the Northern Territory.
Woop Woop	An imaginary town in a far off place.

Some More Strange Australian Place Names:

- **Bong Bong (NSW)** – Aboriginal for out of sight.
- **Tittybong (VIC)** – a country town in Victoria.
- **Yorkey's Knob (QLD)** – named after a fisherman's nickname, Yorkey.
- **Fannie Bay (NT)** – named after the daughter of an explorer's sponsor.
- **Delicate Nobby (NSW)** – a camping area on the NSW coast.
- **Koolyanobbing (WA)** – Aboriginal for place of large, hard rocks.
- **Watanobbi (NSW)** – Aboriginal for hill surrounded by water.
- **Humpty Doo** – possibly an English version of the Aboriginal 'Umdidu' or 'resting place.'
- **Iron Knob** – based on the fact that iron ore is mined there.

Chapter Two:

A Brief History of Australia

How Did Australia Get Here?

Australia was once part of prehistoric super-continent Pangaea and the more southerly Gondwanaland, approximately 100 million years ago, but after a few million years the continent of Australia eventually broke away and became the isolated continent it is today.

The first inhabitants of Australia were the Aboriginal people who, way, way back, migrated from Africa. The seas were much lower than they are today so Aboriginal people walked and island-hopped from Southeast Asia, to Papua New Guinea and then onto Australia. Scientists debate the exact time when Aboriginal people crossed to Australia with some scientists putting it as far as 100000 years ago, while others put it between 40000 and 60000 years ago.

Aboriginal people have a different explanation as to how they came to Australia. Aboriginal people believe they have always been here. Aboriginal people believe in the Dreamtime (the time before anything else).

The Dreaming: The Story of the Rainbow Serpent

Way back in the Dreamtime there were no animals, no birds, no trees or plants nor were there any hills or mountains. Back in the Dreamtime there were only people.

Australia was flat.

There was a great Rainbow Serpent, Goorialla, who awoke and, not seeing any people, he set off to find his own people. He started in the south and slithered his way all the way north, as far as Cape York. There he stopped and created a tremendous red mountain called Narallullgan. Still not finding his people, Goorialla stopped and listened for them but he heard nothing more than people speaking in strange tongues.

'This is not my country', Goorialla thought to himself, 'I must continue on and find my own people'.

Goorialla slithered on from Narallullgan and the twists and turns of his tremendous body created a deep gorge. The giant snake continued north and stopped every evening to listen for his people but he could not hear them so he travelled for many more days, his slithering creating more of the creeks and rivers.

Then one day Goorialla came to the place of two rivers. Lifting his head to the sky he suddenly heard singing. Realising these people spoke his language, Goorialla said to himself, 'These are my people! They are holding a big Bora!' (A Bora is the name both to an initiation ceremony of Indigenous Australians, and to the site on which the initiation is performed).

Manoeuvring himself closer and closer he hid himself behind some bushes. For hours and hours he watched his people before deciding to reveal himself. When they realised he was there they welcomed him warmly.

'You men are not dressed in the right fashion nor are you dancing the right way,' Goorialla said to the men. 'Watch me and I will show you how to dress and to dance correctly.'

And he did, and the men copied him until they were tired.

In the sky above the dark, grey clouds started to gather. The thunder rumbled and the people hurriedly built humpies (small huts made from leaves and branches) for shelter.

Everybody had a shelter, everyone that is, except for the Bil-Bil or Rainbow Lorikeet brothers, so they asked their grandmother, the Star Woman.

'Can't you see my humpy is full of dogs? I have no room for you. I am sorry. I cannot help you boys.'

The Bil-Bil brothers tried several more humpies but none of the people had any room to spare. Then the brothers came to Goorialla's humpy but he was fast asleep and snoring loudly.

The rain became heavier and heavier as the Bil-Bil brothers sought shelter but to no avail. Rushing back to Goorialla's humpy the boys cried out to him, 'Goorialla! The rain is getting heavier and heavier. Please give us some shelter!'

Goorialla awoke.

'Alright, you wait, I will make my humpy bigger,' he said, 'but the only place I can give you shelter is inside my mouth'.

With a tremendous yawn he widened his mouth, the Bil-Bil brothers rushed inside whereupon Goorialla immediately swallowed them.

Fearing the reaction of the people he left immediately and travelled north to the great mountain, Bora-Bunaru.

The next morning, with the storm cleared, the people began to emerge from their humpies. They searched everywhere for the Bil-Bil brothers but they could not find them, they asked each other who had given the boys shelter but no one knew who had. They searched and searched for the Bil-Bil brothers but when they saw Goorialla's tracks they knew that he had swallowed the brothers.

The men quickly snatched up their spears and hurried after Goorialla. Goorialla came to the mountain that towered into the sky as far as the eye could see. He slithered and crawled his way up the cliff and, when he reached the top, he quickly fell asleep, the Bil-Bil brothers still inside his belly.

Following close behind the men with the spears were the rest of the people and soon they all reached the base of Bora-Bunaru.

First, the men attempted to scale the cliff: emu, turkey, brolga, possum, tortoise, and barramundi. Again and again they tried to climb, but each time they fell. That was until the Wangoo, the tree goanna brothers, came along. Gurrinja the Emu said to them, 'it's impossible! We cannot climb this steep mountain!' The Wangoo brothers said, 'it is not impossible! We will climb and climb! We will save the Bil-Bil boys!'

The Wangoo brothers tied together some cords to make a rope. They threw the rope up the side of the mountain and began to climb and climb. For days and days, nights and nights, the Wangoo brothers climbed. When they reached the top they found Goorialla coiled up, fast asleep and snoring.

Silently, they crept closer and closer, when they were right next to Goorialla the older brother said, 'we will cut him open. You start down there and I will start here.'

The brother cut and cut until they reached the Bil-Bil boys. When they peered inside Goorialla's great body they saw they Bil-Bil boys had changed into beautiful parrots with all the colours of the Rainbow Serpent. The Wangoo brothers said, 'you can come out. You are now Rainbow Lorikeets with wings and can fly away.'

The Bil-Bil brothers stretched their wings and flew away.

Goorialla began to stir and the Wangoo brothers ran back down the mountain. Goorialla did not wake but continued to snore and snore until a cool wind blew through his empty stomach.

'Wait!' he said. 'Something is wrong here!'

He looked about and realised he had been cut and his dinner stolen.

Goorialla became angry and worked himself into a great rage. He began to thrash about with fury, his long red tongue flashing like lightning. The great mountain shook and thundered as Goorialla tore it apart with his anger until parts of the mountain began to fall, forming the hills and mountains that we see today.

All the people were terrified of the thunder of the mountain as Goorialla knocked it to pieces. Some were killed by flying stones, others ran away to hide, turning themselves into all the kinds of animals: birds, insects and plant life that live in the country today.

That is how it all happened back in the Dreamtime. When Goorialla's anger was spent there was only small hills left to remind us of the great mountain, Bora-Bunaru.

Goorialla went down and disappeared into the ocean, where he remains to this day. Now the remaining people have to look after all the animals, all the living things which were men and women in the beginning but who were too afraid of old Goorialla to remain as people.

The shooting star racing across the sky at night is the eye of Goorialla watching everybody and, after the rain, you will see his spirit in the sky. This is the reason why he is called Goorialla the Rainbow Serpent.

For an excellent animated version of the story of the Rainbow Serpent visit, *www.youtube.com/watch?v=2vh6moD9ZOU*.

What's In a Name?

'Australia', derives from the Latin, 'Terra Australis', meaning 'The Great Southern Land' but the final name for this great nation of ours has actually come down to us through a long process. For centuries European mapmakers and scientists began to hypothesise that because there was a large landmass to the north of the world then there must be a large continent in the south that must exist in order to 'balance' the world. This they called Terra Australis Incognita or The Great Hidden Southern Land. Later names included the Dutch name, New Holland, which the Europeans kept until the arrival of the British. The British initially referred to the whole country as New South Wales, with the exception of Tasmania, which retained its Dutch name, Van Diemen's Land.

Finding the Hidden Continent...

Once Europeans developed the technology to sail around the world the first European explorers to be near Australia were the Dutch.

1606 - The first European to chart the Australian coastline was Willem Jansz, on his ship the *Duyfken* (Little Dove). He surveyed the coastline around the Gulf of Carpentaria between the Northern Territory and Queensland. Given that the Dutch mostly landed on the northern and western side of Australia and encountered hostile Aboriginals and some of the harshest terrain (and don't forget some of the world's deadliest snakes) they decided not to claim it for Holland but they did give Australia its first name, New Holland.

1616 – The first European to set foot on Australian soil was the Dutchman, Dirk Hartog, who landed his ship, the *Eendracht*, on, what is now called Dirk Hartog Island near Shark Bay in Western Australia. To commemorate his landing, Hartog erected a pewter plate (taken by a later French explorer back to France, then given to Holland, then back to Australia, then back to the Rijksmuseum in Amsterdam.)

1628–29 – A series of Dutchman either landed or were shipwrecked on the Australian coast but one of the interesting stories is that of François Pelsaert – the *Batavia*. The *Batavia* was a brand new ship that was shipwrecked off the coast of Western Australia and the tale of it is an amazing story of mutiny and murder.

1642-44 – Abel Tasman chartered the southern coastline of Australia and he claimed Tasmania (which he named Van Diemen's Land after the then governor-general of the Dutch East Indies Company). Tasman then continued on to New Zealand and then onto some of the Pacific Islands.

The Dutch East Indies Company and the Dutch themselves lost some of their prestige and power as a European nation and, in their place, the British and French rose to prominence and, hence, they became the next nationalities to explore Australia.

1688 – William Dampier, on the *Cygnet*, explored the northwest coast of Australia and was the first Englishman to float the idea of a British exploration of the continent. He later returned in 1699 with orders from the Admiralty to explore more of New Holland. He managed to chart more of the coast but his ship needed repairs and he could not complete his work.

1768 – Louis Antoine de Bougainville was the first Frenchman to sail near to Australia, he wanted to claim the east coast of New Holland and claim it for his nation. However, he encountered the Great Barrier Reef and could not make landfall. Instead he was forced north and found the island near New Guinea, which now bears his name, Bougainville Island.

1770 – Knowing the stories and accounts of the Dutch explorers that came before him, Captain James Cook sailed through the Pacific Ocean wanting to track the transit of Venus in the clear skies of the southern hemisphere but also to claim any lands he may come across for England. Cook landed in Botany Bay in modern day Sydney, and claimed Australia for the British.

The First Fleet: The Birth of Modern Australia

Britain, at the time of Cook's discovery, had made it pretty much a crime to do anything and, as a consequence, their prisons filled rapidly. To solve the problem they began using hulks on the Thames as a prison. But these too became full.

The solution: send their 'criminals' overseas.

America was the first dumping ground, but after the War of Independence England needed to find a new place for their criminals. Cooks' discovery came at a perfect time. It gave Britain a new continental prison.

On the 13th of May 1787, a fleet of 11 ships set sail from Portsmouth, England. Led by Captain Arthur Phillip, this historic convoy, which later became known as the First Fleet, carried officers, crew, marines and their families, and convicts from Britain to a distant and little known land on the far side of the world.

It took more than 250 days to get to their new home, but finally more than 1000 settlers arrived in Port Jackson.

The Aboriginal people from the area, the Eora, must have got an awful shock when they saw eleven ships and white sails in Sydney Harbour. The locals thought the men on the sails were possums!

Later Explorations

1788 – Jean-François de Galaup, comte de Lapérouse, was a scientific explorer who greatly admired the voyages and work and wanted to complete Cook's work. Appointed by Louis XVI, Lapérouse was also under instructions to complete maps, create trading contacts and to improve French scientific collections. Lapérouse travelled the world and arrived in Australia just after Arthur Phillip and the First Fleet. Relations between the French and British were cordial. Lapérouse left after six weeks in Australia and mysteriously disappeared in the Indian Ocean on his way back to France.

1795-1803 – George Bass and Matthew Flinders circumnavigated Tasmania, confirming it to be an island, and then Flinders went on to become the first European to circumnavigate the entire island of Australia.

1801 – Nicolas Baudin conducted a surveying and scientific mission mapping the southwest coast of Australia. He discovered some 2500 unknown species and had friendly encounters with the Aboriginal people. He also engaged in a race with Flinders to be the first one to map the entirety of Australia.

1813 – Gregory Blaxland, William Lawson and William Charles Wentworth crossed the Blue Mountains, west of Sydney. The mountains had, thus far, formed an impenetrable barrier to what the early settlers believed to be rich grazing lands in the interior of the country. Blaxland, Lawson and Wentworth followed the ridgelines and found a path across.

1860–61 – Robert O'Hara Burke and William John Wills were two of numerous explorers who had attempted to find their way into the interior of Australia, but for almost one hundred years had failed. In one of the most famous exploration stories in Australian history, Burke and Wills led an expedition of 19 men. The party was attempting to cross from Melbourne to the Gulf of Carpentaria; a distance of 3250 kilometres (2000 miles).

They managed to reach the Gulf but Burke and Wills died on the return leg of the journey, only one man, John King, managed to successfully return home.

Important Events in Australia's History

The Eureka Stockade and Rebellion – 1854

In the 1850s Australia was in the midst of a gold rush. People flocked from all over the world to strike it rich. The British government knew a good thing when they saw it so charged extensively for Miner's Licenses. This led to growing civil disobedience on the goldfields, which consequently led to more conflict between the miners and the authorities.

In 1854, the miners rebelled and built themselves a stockade. The Colonial forces laid siege and, in the ensuing battle, 27 miners and soldiers were killed.

Whilst their battle was lost, the Australian people had sympathy for the 'diggers' and their ideas of challenging authority and sticking by their mates earned them respect. Many of the soldiers who would fight in subsequent wars, such as the Boer War, were miners too so the name 'diggers' stuck.

The word 'diggers' is now mostly associated with First World War soldiers but the ideas of equality and mateship still live on.

Ned Kelly – 1878–1880

Ned Kelly is, depending on your point of view, either a national hero or one of Australia's most famous criminals. Ned Kelly, a man of good Irish stock, is one of Australia's most renowned bushrangers (someone who robs banks and stage coaches and then disappears back into the bush). Kelly, and his gang, committed numerous crimes and murders but Kelly argued that the authorities were the criminals and the murderers.

Kelly's last stand took place at the town of Glenrowan, Victoria, on the 28th of June 1880. Dressed in his famous suit of homemade metal armour and helmet, Kelly made his last stand. He was eventually shot in the leg, arrested and placed on trial for the murder of three policemen. He was convicted and hung. His last words were, reportedly, 'such is life.'

Despite his crimes, Kelly's stance against the overbearing authorities has led to him gaining hero status.

Women in South Australia gain the right to vote – 1894

The suffragette movement in Australia extends as far back as 1854. These ladies put out leaflets, organised meetings and petitioned politicians for the right to vote. South Australia was the first state to give women the right to vote in 1893. After the birth of Australia as a nation in 1901, women across the country gained the right to vote and, eventually, the right to stand for political election. Australia's first female elected to parliament was Edith Cowan in the Western Australian Legislative Assembly in 1921.

Federation – 1901

Australia started as a collection of six separate colonies, often with different money, tax systems, defence forces and railroads. While there was much debate about whether Federation (joining as a federally governed country) was the best path to follow, it was decided, by referendum, that federating was mutually beneficial. Things such as taxation and defence were passed to the Federal government.

Interestingly, New Zealand and Fiji were asked if they wanted to be part of a broader, Pacific Federation but they declined.

On the 1st of January 1901, the separate states of Australia became the Commonwealth of Australia. Australia remains a constitutional monarchy, in that, we have a constitution to set out the basic rights of our citizens but Queen Elizabeth II stills remains as the monarch of Australia.

Anzac Landing – April 25th, 1915

If a foreigner asked an Aussie about the birth of our country, a lot of Australians would state the landing at Gallipoli, Turkey. It was here where Australians, as a nation, were thrust into the heat of battle. The soldiers' brave exploits and courage under fire was when Australians were able to prove themselves to the rest of the world and stake their place as a modern nation.

For more information on the ANZAC tradition see page 100.

Phar Lap – 1930

Phar Lap, whilst he was born in New Zealand, was trained in Australia and earned his status as a legend for his racing exploits in this country. Winning the biggest races in Australia, chiefly the Melbourne Cup. Phar Lap's career was cut short when he died in 1932. There are still several theories as to the cause of death, including that he had been poisoned. Phar Lap was considered to have a 'big heart' as a racehorse but, in fact, he actually did have a big heart. It weighed 6.2 kg, compared to that of a normal horse's heart at 3.2kg. Phar Lap became a national icon due to the hope and excitement he brought to the nation during the worst times of the Depression.

The Fall of Singapore – 1942

Prior to 1942, Singapore was considered to be an impregnable fortress that, despite the Japanese army's rapid move through Southeast Asia in the Second World War, the city would not fall and Australia would be safe. However, this could not have been further from the truth. Not only did Singapore fall, but it fell quickly and nearly 100000 Allied soldiers were taken prisoner. Britain, fighting Hitler in Europe and unable to offer any more aid, Australia looked to the United States. This led to our current alliance with the United States.

The Bombing of Darwin – 1942
Australia, to this day, has never had an invading foreign army set foot on Australian soil; we have only been attacked by air, and by sea by the Japanese in the Second World War. The first, and largest, of these attacks came on the 19th of February 1942, when the Japanese bombed Darwin, the capital of the Northern Territory. A total number of 235 Australian soldiers and civilians were killed and more than 300 were wounded, 30 Allied aircraft were destroyed and 8 ships were sunk, with more than 25 damaged. Over 100 air raids were carried out on the northern parts of Australia, including Townsville and Broome, but the Japanese never landed troops.

Australia in the Vietnam War – 1962–1975
Fearing the spread of communism through Southeast Asia, Australia fought with the United States in Vietnam. Despite Australia's ANZAC tradition the veterans of this war were not treated with the same respect as previous veterans. Famous Aussie songs such as *I Was Only 19* by Redgum and tireless campaigning not only brought these men the respect they deserve but also highlighted the seriousness of Post-Traumatic Stress Disorder.

Referendum for Aboriginal Citizenship – 1967
Prior to 1967, Aboriginal people were considered to be part of the native flora and fauna (i.e. they were not considered people). When the British arrived they considered the land Terra Nullius, or land without people, and this led to how Aboriginal people were viewed. Aboriginal people had long protested for equal rights and, on the 27th of May, a referendum was held to change the Australian constitution. Aboriginal people were not without support. The referendum resulted in a 90.77 per cent 'yes' vote.

Eddie Mabo – 1992

Eddie 'Koiki' Mabo was an Indigenous man from the Murray Islands in the north of Queensland who fought to get his island back after he discovered that the Australian government technically owned it. Mabo's efforts to reclaim his land went all the way to the High Court of Australia where he was successful. This decision forever changed the Land Rights laws in Australia but, unfortunately, Mabo died a few months prior and never lived to enjoy his victory.

Bali Bombings – 2002

Bali has long been a favourite holiday destination for Australians but, in 2002, the idyllic location became a place of absolute horror. On the 12th of October, Al-Qaeda members placed bombs near the US Consulate and several Western nightclubs. The bomb that most affected Australians was the one that exploded in the *Sari* Club. A total of 88 Australians were killed. In all, the co-ordinated bombings were responsible for the deaths of 202 people.

Apology for the Stolen Generations – 2008

In modern Australia much has been done to improve relations between Indigenous and non-Indigenous Australians. We call this process 'Reconciliation'. One the most significant moments in the reconciliation process was the apology speech given by Prime Minister, Kevin Rudd, in 2008. The move was one of the biggest in Australia's history and went a long way to healing the rift between black and white people in Australia.

Black Saturday Bushfires – 2009

Bushfires are a natural part of Australian life. In fact, many of our native plants need bushfires to regenerate and the Aboriginal people have long used deliberate fires as a hunting method. Australians accept bushfires as a part of life but in 2009 one of the worst series of bushfires hit Victoria. Soaring heat (near 45 degrees Celsius) and inclement wind conditions created the perfect weather for fires. A total number of 173 Australians were killed in the fires and a further 414 were injured.

The Biggest Controversies in Australian History

William Bligh and the Rum Rebellion – 1808

Many countries around the world have had numerous military coups to
overthrow the government of the time. Australia, however, has only had one.
On 'Australia Day', the 26th of January 1808, the military overthrew the then
Governor of Australia, William Bligh, in a bloodless coup. Major George
Johnston of the New South Wales Corps (or Rum Corps) headed to the military
barracks and declared to his men that he was going to assume control of the
colony. The event has now become known as the Rum Rebellion. The colony
of New South Wales did not have a solid currency of notes and coins so trade
worked on a barter system. The most popular form of currency was rum and the
monopoly on this was controlled by the soldiers and their commanders. Several
governors tried, in vain, to break the monopoly but too many powerful men,
such as John Macarthur, were not prepared to lose their power and influence.

The Disappearance of Prime Minister Harold Holt – 1966

In a bizarre case involving the leader of the nation, the 17th Prime Minister of
Australia, Harold Holt, went for a morning swim at Cheviot Beach on the 17th
December 1967, near Portsea, Victoria. Holt was never seen again, presumed
drowned. Holt's contribution to Australian politics came from the time before
he was Prime Minister, firstly, as Immigration Minister where he pushed for the
relaxation of the White Australia Policy and, secondly, pushing for decimal
currency during his time as Treasurer. In a typically Australian ironic fashion,
there are swim centres in Victoria named in his honour.

The Whitlam Dismissal – 1975

The Prime Minister in 1975 was Gough Whitlam, he was a controversial figure
in Australian politics. Whitlam's Labour government had been elected in 1972
with a small majority in the House of Representatives, but with the Opposition
controlling the Senate. In 1975, the Australian parliament reached an impasse.
Neither house, the upper (Senate) nor lower (House of Representatives), could

pass laws and the Governor-General of Australia, John Kerr, appealed to the Queen (who, as stated earlier, is still the official head of Australia) and, on the 11th of November, Whitlam was dismissed. The reasons for the dismissal and the legitimacy of it still remain hotly debated topics. The Whitlam dismissal remains the only time the Queen has intervened in Australian politics.

The Chamberlain Case – 1980

Made famous by the movie, *Evil Angels*, the Lindy Chamberlain case is one of the greatest controversies in modern Australia. On the 17th of August 1980, the Chamberlain family were camping near Uluru. Michael and Lindy Chamberlain awoke to find their two and a half year old baby, Azaria, missing. All that remained was some bloodied baby clothes.

When the media got hold of this, a circus ensued.

Chamberlain claimed, now famously, 'a dingo's got my baby.'

Authorities at the time stated that this was the 'most likely' cause but controversy raged over the next seven years (and beyond) as to whether this was indeed the case or whether the Chamberlains had murdered their daughter.

A Royal Commission (the highest legal investigation in Australia) ruled in 1987 that, again, a dingo was the 'most likely' cause of death but debate still continued.

It was not until 2012 that the Chamberlains were fully cleared.

Local Knowledge: The Mutiny on the Bounty

Governor William Bligh, whilst being deposed during the Rum Rebellion, is probably most famous for the Mutiny on the Bounty. The story takes place in 1789 and popular history says that Bligh's men wanted to return to the idyllic lifestyle they had encountered on the island of Tahiti and were angered by Bligh's refusal to do so and his supposed harsh treatment of them.

The mutiny was led by Fletcher Christian and they set Bligh and the men loyal to him adrift in the Pacific Ocean.

The mutineers themselves settled in both Tahiti and the small island of Pitcairn (where their descendants still live today) while Bligh managed to navigate his small rowboat (only 7 metres in length) some 6700 kilometres (4100 miles) to Timor in the Dutch East Indies.

When Bligh returned to England and reported the incident the British Government sent a ship, the *Pandora*, to find the mutineers. Many were taken prisoner and, after a shipwreck on the Barrier Reef, the remaining men were tried. Some were hanged, some pardoned and some imprisoned.

The Symbols of Australia

The Australian Flag

There has been much controversy in recent years about the Australian flag with many people discussing whether we should change it to remove the Union Jack.

Our flag has a blue background, with the Union Jack on the top-left hand side and the Southern Cross on the right hand side. The Union Jack reflects our British heritage and the Southern Cross represents our geographical location, given it is a star constellation only visible in the Southern Hemisphere. The Federation Star, the largest star on the lower-left side of the flag, has seven points representing the six states of Australia and the territories.

The Australian flag was first used in 1901, the year of Federation. It symbolises everything about Australia and questions about changing it have been shouted down because many of our soldiers have fought for that flag.

The flag is, of course, flown at half-mast when important people in the country pass away and important soldiers or other dignitaries have their coffin draped in the flag. Although the Flag was adopted in 1901, it did not receive royal approval (hence becoming official) until 1954.

The Aboriginal Flag

After being granted the right to be treated as citizens in the 1967 referendum, Aboriginal people began large-scale Land Rights movements to claim land

taken from them by European settlers. As part of
their drive for further rights, a Luritja man from
Central Australia, Harold Thomas, designed the first
Aboriginal flag. By his own definition, Mr Thomas,
explained the symbolic meaning of the flag as being:

Black: Represents the Aboriginal people of
Australia.

Red: Represents the red earth, the red ochre and a spiritual relation to
the land.

Yellow: Represents the sun, the giver of life and protector.

The flag was officially adopted by the Australian government as an official
'Flag of Australia' in 1995.

The Australian Coat of Arms

The Australian official coat of arms carries a
kangaroo on the right hand side with an emu on
the left. The reasons these two animals appear is,
not only because they are national symbols, but
because neither animal is able to walk or move
backwards and this, in turn, is representative
of how we see ourselves as Australians and as
a nation.

The two animals have their paws/claws on a shield which carries the
symbols of the six states and the seven-starred symbol of the Australian states
appear above this.

Golden Wattle

The National flower of Australia is the Golden Wattle and the reason this
was chosen is because, when in full bloom, the plant displays the two national
colours of green and gold.

State Floral Emblems

New South Wales	The Waratah
Australian Capital Territory	Royal Bluebell
Northern Territory	Sturt's Desert Rose
Queensland	Cooktown Orchid
South Australia	Sturt's Desert Pea
Tasmania	Tasmanian Blue Gum
Victoria	Common Heath
Western Australia	Red and Green Kangaroo Paw

The Opal

Australia's national gemstone in the opal and much of the world's supply comes from the Outback, South Australian town, of Coober Pedy. Coober Pedy is, in itself, rather interesting because many people in the town, due to the excessive Outback heat, live underground. Even Coober Pedy's church is underground.

The opal is a rainbow-coloured gemstone. The world's largest opal is the Olympic Australis, found in 1956, its name was in honour of the fact that the Olympics were being held in Melbourne at the time. The gem is valued at AUD$2.5 million.

The Southern Cross

An archetypal Australian symbol, the Southern Cross is a series of stars in the Crux constellation. There are five stars in the Southern Cross – Alpha, Beta, Delta, Gamma and Epsilon Crucis. These stars are estimated to be between 10 and 20 million years old. The closest of them is 88 light-years from earth, the furthest 364 light-years.

Chapter Three:

Who are the Aussies?

A Multicultural Melting Pot

Australia's multicultural landscape is proving to be as diverse as ever following the release of the 2011 Census of Population and Housing data by the Australian Bureau of Statistics (ABS).

Almost a quarter (24.6 per cent) of Australia's population was born overseas and near enough to half of all Aussies (43.1 per cent) have at least one overseas-born parent.

It is no surprise, given our British heritage, to find that the largest number of immigrants to Australia is from the United Kingdom (20.8 per cent). It is also no surprise to find that the next largest number of immigrants to Australia is from our nearest neighbour, New Zealand (9.1 per cent).

The next two highest numbers of immigrants come from the world's two largest countries, China accounting for 6 per cent of immigration and India, 5.6 per cent.

White Australia Policy

Australia, given its British heritage, instituted a policy in the early 20th century that meant unless you met strict guidelines of being 'white', you were not allowed to migrate to Australia. Migrants living in Australia, particularly those of Chinese heritage, were subjected to strict testing. People who were not considered 'white' had to undergo a dictation test, however, the test could be given in any European language. Plainly, many immigrants failed the test and were deported. Moves to remove the White Australia Policy began after the Second World War and it was finally abolished in 1973.

Waves of Immigration

The first people to migrate to Australia were the Aboriginals. Australia's Indigenous population at the time of the arrival of the Europeans is estimated to be between 300, 000 and 1 million. This figure went down with the introduction of smallpox and other European diseases but the Indigenous population is now estimated to be nearly 700, 000.

From the arrival of just over 1000 people with the first settlers, Australia's population grew to over a million people by 1858, two million by 1878, 4 million by 1906, 8 million by 1951 and 20 million by 2006.

During the Gold Rush of the 1850s, many migrants, particularly from China, came to Australia.

After the Second World War, Australian politicians realised we needed to grow our population and instituted the policy of 'populate or perish.' The £10 policy allowed many British people to pay the ten pounds for a boat fare to migrate to Australia. Australia also had waves of other Europeans, fleeing war-torn Europe, including many Jewish refugees; unfortunately they were not always welcomed with open arms.

The Australian government, continuing with the population or perish mentality, wanted to expand our migration laws to include non-whites but they had to be of European heritage. Australia's growing population, particularly in New South Wales, also meant that the authorities had to increase the power and electricity supply. One of the most ambitious projects, the Snowy Mountains Scheme, was devised.

The Scheme involved using the alpine water from the Snowy River to create a hydroelectric plant. Realising that there were not enough workers to successfully complete the project, the government softened their stance, but only slightly, to allow 'other' Europeans.

Southern Europeans (Greeks, Italians, Yugoslavs) formed the majority of the new workers imported into Australia but they were often referred to as 'wogs' (nevertheless, they now play a vital role in modern, multicultural Australia).

Under Prime Minister, Gough Whitlam, our immigration policies further expanded. As stated, Whitlam abolished the White Australia policy in 1973, which coincided with an escalation in the Vietnam War, and the first waves of boat people began. Australia also felt a responsibility to take in refugees from the war-torn country and many Vietnamese people now called Australia home. Many other Asian migrants came to Australia, which enriched our culture and continued the path of our nation becoming more engaged with our Asian neighbours (plus they introduced great food!).

In the late 20th and earlier 21st centuries, the Middle East had dictatorial regimes in Iraq and Afghanistan, anyone who disagreed with the governments of Saddam Hussein or the Taliban were tortured, persecuted and murdered. Fleeing such horrendous living conditions, the next wave of migration to Australia came, mostly, from these two countries.

After the turn of the millennium, with other conflicts arising around the world, the face of Australia immigration has changed once again. With conflicts in the Darfur region of Sudan and in other parts of Africa, the 21st Century wave of migration is seeing many more people of African origin choosing to call Australia home.

Local Knowledge: The 'Boat People' Controversy

Australia prides itself on being a multicultural country but one of the major controversies in modern Australia, something that heavily divides the people, is the issue of 'boat people' and illegal immigration. Given that Australia is an island the only way to illegally enter Australia, apart from on a plane, is by boat. The people coming in by boat are generally referred to as 'asylum seekers,' in that, they are escaping persecution and are seeking asylum in Australia.

Many Aussies believe that the claims of asylum seekers are genuine and that these people are, indeed, refugees. Their argument is that Australia has signed international agreements to take in refugees so it is only right that we process these people as such and allow them entry into the country.

On the reverse side of the argument, many other Aussies believe that these asylum claims are not genuine and that boat people are nothing more than 'queue jumpers'. Their argument is that, by entering illegally, these people are taking the place of other migrants who go through the proper channels to move to Australia.

The greatest controversy regarding this issue was the Tampa Affair. Most illegal boats are of very poor quality and in August 2001, 438 refugees were saved by the Norwegian freighter, the MV *Tampa*, after their ship had sunk. The problem was that the Norwegian ship picked up the asylum seekers in international waters and the captain, fearing for the health of the refugees, carried them into Australian waters.

The Howard government considered that, under international law, the asylum seekers should be taken to the nearest international port, which was in Indonesia. The Howard government also ordered Australian Special Forces to board the ship to assess the medical conditions of the refugees, eventually ordering the ship to return to international waters.

Norway considered this to be an outrage and that Australia was not meeting its international human rights obligations.

Some of the refugees were later settled in Australia, others in New Zealand and others, who were not considered legitimate refugees, were sent back to their country of origin.

What Makes An Aussie?

It is a difficult question to ask what makes an Aussie, we are so multicultural we now have Aussies from nearly 200 countries. Despite our traditional British heritage and our somewhat racist policies, Australia now prides itself on having people from all types of backgrounds that consider themselves 'Aussies'.

Within 70 years Australia has transformed itself into what many of us call a 'multicultural melting pot'. We have Serbs, Croats, Brits, Irish, Scots, Iraqis, Afghanis, Indians, Chinese, Sudanese, Sri Lankans… the list goes on.

The Original Aussies

History of the Aboriginal People

Aboriginal people have lived in Australia anywhere between 40000 and 60000 years. When the British arrived in Australia they did not understand the Aboriginal way of life. The Aboriginal people (an estimated 500 different tribal groups who spoke 700 spoken languages) were nomadic and moved from place to place only taking what they needed and never overusing the available resources. Given that they saw no sign of Aboriginal people cultivating the land the British did not see them as civilised and therefore declared the land Terra Nullius.

Bennelong

Bennelong was a senior member of the Eora nation, the first Aboriginal group to come into contact with Arthur Phillip and other British settlers. Phillip was under instruction from King George III to establish cordial relations with the 'natives'. Phillip's attempts to do so were thwarted because the Eora people easily evaded the newcomers. Phillip resorted to kidnap and after the first man they captured, Arabanoo, died from smallpox they captured Bennelong.

Bennelong spent six months with the British, each man learning the ways of the other man's people before escaping. Bennelong initiated contact with Phillip and took him to Manly where he was speared (as retribution for British kidnappings). With his debt paid, the relationship between Bennelong and Phillip grew and Bennelong learnt to speak English and lived amongst the colonists, dressing and acting like them. In 1792, Bennelong went to Britain, returning to Australia in 1795. Bennelong resumed his important position amongst his people as well as helping the next British governor, Governor Hunter. He died in 1813.

Pemulway

Pemulway was an Aboriginal resistance leader who led a guerrilla war campaign against the British. Born in 1750, Pemulway was a member of the Bidjigal clan, part of the Eora people. Pemulway's resistance began when he speared a man named Macintyre in retaliation for Macintyre's killing of Aboriginal people. Governor Arthur Phillip had long considered the Bidjigal people troublesome and, given Macintyre was Phillip's gamekeeper, he ordered six of the Bidjigal be captured or killed.

The British, not knowing the land and weighed down by their equipment, failed in their attempts. Between 1792 and 1802, Pemulway conducted a series of raids on farms and settlements. He was wounded and shot several times as well as being captured but still managed to escape, the British began to believe he was invincible. However, Pemulway was shot and killed in 1802.

His was beheaded and his skull was sent to England. This causes great controversy to this day as the Bidjigal people are still petitioning the British government to have Pemulway's head returned to his people.

The Black Wars

The Black Wars were a series of conflicts between the Tasmanian Aboriginals and the British people between 1828 and 1832. What began as competition over resources and of Aboriginal people taking revenge at the kidnapping of their women and children, led to a concerted campaign by the British to remove the Aboriginals from the island altogether. Roving parties of soldiers scoured the island and any Aboriginal considered to be resisting was shot.

By 1830, the government was offering a bounty of £5 per adult and £2 per child for each Aboriginal caught alive. An ambitious 'round-up' called the Black Line occurred. Men and soldiers formed a huge line and 1000 of them swept the countryside looking for any Aboriginals they could find.

The Aborigines, realising the extent of the opposition to them, eventually agreed to be re-settled to Flinders Island.

There is debate about whether the British actions during this time constituted genocide but what is beyond doubt, is that the Tasmanian Aboriginals were pushed to the point of extinction. To this day, some argue that there are no Tasmanian Aboriginals left, the woman Truganini, (c. 1812–8 May 1879) is widely considered to be the last full blood Aboriginal Tasmanian, however many Tasmanian Aboriginals surviving today may have something to say about this.

The Myall Creek Massacre

On the 10th of June 1838, dozens of unarmed, Indigenous people, from the Kamilaroi people, were sheltering on Charles Kilmeister's farm after he had invited them on to his property. A dozen white stockmen, after tying the Aboriginals together, led them to a gully almost a kilometre away. Approximately, 28 old men, women and children were slaughtered. At the later trial of the stockmen, testimony was given that the women and children were beheaded while the old men were forced to run a gauntlet of sword-wielding men on horses and were slowly hacked to pieces. Even Kilmeister was involved.

After roaming the countryside for two more days looking for more Aboriginals to kill the group returned to Myall Creek and burned the remains of the massacred people.

Of the 12 men who participated in the massacre, only 11 went to trial and only seven were eventually convicted and hanged.

The Stolen Generations

A dark chapter in Australian history is the Stolen Generations. Between 1909 and 1969 it was official government policy to remove half-caste and lighter skinned Aboriginal children from their families and to place them with white families or in Christian missions.

There is much debate as to the government and various organisations involved motives. Some argue that it was an attempt to 'breed' the Aboriginal out. Other people argue that, given the destruction caused by white settlement to the Aboriginal populations, the Stolen Generations were an attempt to save a 'dying' race.

The official policies of the various governments around the country were referred to in terms of 'paternalism', 'assimilation' and 'protectionism', illustrating that despite whatever motives they had, the people involved genuinely believed they were doing the right thing by the Aboriginals.

Regardless, the psychological effects it had on the Aboriginal children were immense. Many of the children of the Stolen Generations were taken to places miles and miles away from their traditional lands, never to see their families again.

Local Knowledge: Some Important Aboriginal Traditions You Need To Know

The most iconic Aboriginal tradition is, of course, the Didgeridoo (a long, hollowed out piece of wood), the boomerang and dot paintings. What many visitors do not understand is that the use of the 'Didg', as it is colloquially

known, is highly ritualised. Didgeridoos are only supposed to be
played by a man. Additionally, the Didg is a mostly northern Australian
instrument, whereas the boomerang was utilised in the southeast of
Australia even though they have become national Aboriginal icons. The
traditional dot painting associated with Aboriginal art actually originates
from the Aboriginal nations from the central regions of Australia.

It is also important to understand that Aboriginal people are not one
homogenous group. Aboriginal people will refer to their lands as their 'country'
and they will refer to their group of people as their 'nation'. So, even though
modern day Australia is one nation Aborigines consider that they have many
peoples and many countries.

The word "aborigine" (with a little "a") means one of the original native
inhabitants of any country. The word "Aborigine" (with a capital "A") is
used to describe the Indigenous people of Australia. In Australia, many non-
Aboriginal people use the terms "Aboriginal" and "Aboriginals" as singular and
plural nouns for the people. Aborigines describe themselves using the various
words that mean "person" from each of their own different language groups
(tribes). A person from the Sydney region might describe himself or herself as
'Koori', from Darwin as 'Larrakeyah', from northeast Arnhem Land as 'Yolgnu',
and central Australian has Pitjantjatjara, Pintubi etc.

Aborigines have differing views on how their culture should be described.
On the one hand, their people are proud of their culture and want outsiders to
know of it. They have seen the impact of European culture in Australia and
the threat this has to their own culture. Fearing the loss of their knowledge,
both secular and sacred, they have imparted much that was once secret, known
only to the most senior members of their clans, to explorers, missionaries,
pastoralists, interested visitors and anthropologists.

On the other hand, in order to continue their cultural traditions and
maintain law and order, they need some of the secrecy of their initiation rites
and ceremonies kept. This secrecy makes the process meaningful for future
generations. For more information on Aboriginal culture visit:
www.aboriginalculture.com.au.

The Most Famous Aboriginal Word

The most common Aboriginal word travellers from another country would be familiar with would be the word 'kangaroo'. This word comes from Guugu Yimidhirr, the language of the Cooktown region in northern Queensland. Kangaroo or kanguru was a word that Captain James Cook learned from the local Aboriginal people when his ship, the *Endeavour*, needed repairs and Cook and his crew were forced to stop in the area.

The actual word 'kangaroo' only applies to the grey kangaroo but, as James Cook's journeys were the handbook for South Seas travel, Captain Arthur Phillip took what Cook had recorded and mistakenly thought it was a generic Aboriginal word and, so, the first Europeans used it in an attempt to communicate with the Eora people from Sydney. In one of the great historical ironies, the Aboriginals thought it must be an English word and, hence, it stuck.

Some Other Aboriginal Words and Terms

Bunyip – mythical outback creature.
Corroboree – an Aboriginal dance festival.
Deadly – an Aboriginal slang word for great or awesome.
Dingo – a native dog.
Gubba – a non-Aboriginal person.
Kookaburra – an iconic Australian bird known for its laugh.
Koala – in Aboriginal the word means 'no drink'.
Mob – family or a group of people.
Waratah – a stunning red flower.
Yabby – a freshwater crayfish.

The Benefits of Being an Aussie

Aussies, for the most part, are pretty happy with our lot in life and here's why...

1. *We're free to go where we bloody please!*

   Within Australia there is no border controls (about the only thing you can't take across a border is fruit). It's a bit of a long way to anywhere else, apart from New Zealand or Papua New Guinea (which, strangely we need a visa for), but generally us Aussies have a pretty good reputation for ourselves in other countries. Aussies can visit 168 countries and territories visa-free or with visa on arrival, placing us 6th overall in freedom of travel.

2. *We have got no real problems with the neighbours* (except maybe the rugby or the underarm ball!).

   We have our rivalries but we can visit New Zealand and, given our general lack of snow, skiing and snowboarding in New Zealand are high on most Aussies' list. Bali in Indonesia is also another popular Australian tourist destination.

3. *We have way more space than we need.*

   China has approximately 144 people per square kilometre. India has approximately 422 people per square kilometre. Australia has approximately 2.91 people per square kilometres.

4. *Our money won't get destroyed when it gets put through the wash!*

   Australia has polymer (plastic) banks notes (see the **Who's That in Your Wallet?** section for more detail). You can put them through the wash, go for a swim with them in your pocket and they're still all good.

5. *Our Country is, simply put, Paradise.*

   We have the best of every type of environment imaginable. We have coral reefs, beaches, snow, deserts, mountains, and rainforests.

6. *Australians firmly believe in the concept of a 'fair go'.*

   The right to a 'fair go' in Australia is that as long as you are prepared to work hard you should be given the opportunity to excel in whatever field or endeavours you choose. Everybody, whether they are born here or migrate, has the right to a fair go. If you can put in the hard work to make it, then good luck to you!

7. *Everybody is your 'mate'.*

It doesn't matter in Australia if you know someone or not, whether they're male or female, everyone is your mate. The true extent of our concept of helping out a mate comes with one of our very frequent natural disasters (mainly floods and bushfires) when complete strangers help out those in need.

8. *Sunshine.*

Whilst it can get to 50 degrees in parts of Australia and the road is so hot that it melts the soles of your shoes, summer is all about cricket, beers, beaches and barbecues. And, we love it! But, we don't really have a choice; Aussie towns have, on average, 150 sunny days a year.

9. *We don't have a class system.*

Our convict heritage has probably led to this one. We have always had a healthy distaste for authority and the upper classes. Even the richest of Aussies will try and present themselves as larrikins or average people (and so will politicians, even though we know that Aussie politicians are some of the highest paid in the world). It doesn't matter what level of society you are from, as long as you're a good person, then you're okay.

10. *Everybody has to vote.*

If you fail to vote in Australia you get fined ($20). This might not sound like a lot but if it you don't pay it ends up in court and the costs can rise. The fact that everyone has a vote means that everyone is having their own say on the running of our country. This means every Australian has the right to complain about the government!

11. *We have one of the best medical systems in the world.*

A visit to the doctors is free for all Australians. Now, trying to get into the emergency room or elective surgery can be a complete nightmare but serious injuries etc. are generally looked after pretty quickly. We also have the option of paying for extra health care if we so choose to.

12. *Education is free (well, sort of).*

All children are entitled to a free primary and high school education. Higher education, such as University, becomes a little trickier. Technically, it's not free. Whilst you don't have to pay up front, you do have a Higher Education Contribution Scheme (HECS), which you pay off through the course of your working life.

13. *There is no compulsory military service.*

With the exception of the Vietnam War, Australia has never had conscription. Even in the First World War we had a referendum to decide whether or not introduce conscription and the country voted that if you were going to fight in a war then you should not be forced to go. This is not to say that Australians won't fight for their country, hundreds of thousands signed up, voluntarily, for all the major wars.

14. *Your life revolves around the water.*

Even though there might be sharks, stingers and other things that kill you, water is our way of life. In summer, and winter, most Aussies are either swimming, sunbathing or fishing.

15. *We don't do tipping!*

You Americans have fallen down by now but, the truth is, we don't need to tip because our minimum wage is so high ($16.87/ hour)! Tipping is, however, optional. If you think someone's service is well above what is required then you are welcome to tip them.

16. *We have an eclectic political system.*

Whilst Australian politics is dominated by the Liberal (right-wing) and Labor (left-wing) parties we also have many other parties to choose from. In our last national election members of the Motorist Enthusiasts' Party were elected. We also had the Marijuana Smoker' Party and the Sex Party.

17. *Our animals.*

We have the weirdest, strangest, yet cutest animals in the world. True, we also have some of the most deadly, but the cute ones outweigh that!

18. *Everybody loves an Aussie.*

Our laid back lifestyle, our sense of humour, our willingness to treat everyone equally (and, our accent) means, generally, people from other countries love us. This means that when we travel we are treated well.

19. *The public holidays.*

Australia is ranked amongst the top nations for most number of public holidays per year. Depending on which state you live in, we have, on average, 11 public holidays per year. Added to our, on average, 20 days per year annual leave – we have 31 days off work annually. In addition to this, we value people who have to work on this days, so working on a public holiday can get you double the pay!

20. *The community spirit.*

Aussies are a very charitable bunch. Around the country there are always people cooking barbies, selling sausage sandwiches or selling raffle tickets for a chicken in order to raise money for someone who needs it.

Meet Some Aussies: 25 Famous Aussies You Need To Know

Hugh Jackman, Nicole Kidman, Paul Hogan, Peter Allen and the three Hemsworth brothers; Liam, Chris and Luke. These are some of the Aussies people around the world know. The following list, whilst not all inclusive, is so that you may get an idea of some other famous Aussies that may not have received as much worldwide attention. They are in no specific order as to who is the greatest Aussie because to do so would diminish from their achievements and would lead to many arguments!

Richie Benaud (1930-2015)

The voice of cricket in Australia for more than 50 years. Richie Benaud was a former Test batsman and leg-spin bowler who played 63 Test matches for Australia (captain for 28), taking 248 wickets and scoring 2201 runs. Richie's phrases such as, 'super effort that!', 'what a catch!' and 'welcome back to the MCG,' have become everyday catchphrases in Australia.

Errol Flynn (1909-1959)

In the words of a great Aussie band, *Australian Crawl*, 'Oh, Errol! I would give anything, just to be like him!' And why wouldn't they want to be like him, in his time, Errol Flynn was the biggest movie star in the world. A humble boy from Tasmania went to the States and became world-famous for his role in many a romantic swashbuckling film. One of the sexiest film stars of all time he starred in classic movies such as *Robin Hood* and *Captain Blood*. Flynn's later life was plagued with troubles, both physical and financial, but this cannot take away from the fact he was Australia's first, true, Hollywood superstar.

Reg Grundy (1923-)

Reg Grundy played a, sometimes undervalued, role in the spread of Australian culture. Grundy started his media career in radio in the 1950s and went on to create a series of highly successful television programs. Grundy is responsible for well-known television series such as *Neighbours* which has, in turn, spread Aussie culture to the world and created pop-icons such as Kylie Minogue.

Fred Hollows (1929-1993)

Fred spent years traipsing through the Outback restoring sight to Aboriginal people. He then expanded this to helping people in Africa and Asia. Hollows significance goes far beyond giving people their sight; by involving himself in Indigenous peoples' health he brought attention to the poor-state of their health and the lack of medical services. His forays into the developing world also helped promote the importance of international aid.

Sir Henry Parkes (1815-1896)

Sir Henry Parkes is known as the Father of Federation. He was one of the earliest proponents of the Federal Council of the colonies of Australia. Parkes had to fight hard for Federation too; given that many politicians from New South Wales were worried about the effects it would have on the colony. As the leader of the colony he called the Federation Conference in 1890, something that was seen as the first genuine step towards Australia becoming a nation.

Slim Dusty (1927-2003)

The undisputed master of country music in Australia, Slim Dusty (David Gordon Kirkpatrick) is responsible for many classic Australia songs such as *Pub With No Beer* and *Have A Beer With Duncan*. Slim Dusty was an integral part in developing the Outback identity of Australia. Slim received 37 Golden Guitar awards and 2 Australian Recording Industry Association (ARIA) awards, the highest in Australian music. When he died at the age of 76, Slim was working on his 106th album!

Barry Humphries (1935 -)

People from Britain and America may know Barry as one of his alter egos, Dame Edna Everage. Born in Melbourne in 1934, Humphries is considered to be one of Australia's best comedians and scriptwriters. Humphries had many key roles in Australian TV and Cinema before heading to London and the West End. Everage continues to be his biggest success.

Julia Gillard (1961-)

Julia Gillard was the 27th Prime Minister of Australia and our country's first female Prime Minister. Gillard held the office from 2010-2013. Gillard, originally from Wales, moved to Australia in 1966. She went on to be a lawyer, then into politics. She held positions as Minister for Education and Minister for Employment and Workplace Relations, amongst others, before becoming Deputy Leader of the Labor party and, finally, the Leader. Gillard gained a lot of criticism for the way she came to be Prime Minister in that the Labor Party had a leadership spill vote and Gillard was, therefore, not technically elected by the people. The people elected her in 2010, before losing to Tony Abbott in the 2013 elections. Gillard is the second Australian Prime Minister to be born overseas.

Dennis Lillee (1949 -)

Dennis Lillee is often called the most outstanding fast bowler of his generation. Lillee has become a national icon because of the quickness of his bowling but also because he was injured on numerous occasions and undertook a strict fitness regime to get himself back to full strength, an embodiment of the Aussie attitude to life. In his time, Lillee was the highest wicket taker of all time (355 wickets). Lillee now spends his time mentoring young fast bowlers around the world.

Dame Nellie Melba (1861-1931)

Born Helen 'Nellie' Porter Mitchell, Dame Nellie Melba was Australia's first world famous operatic singer. Dame Nellie started her singing career in Melbourne, hence why she took the pseudonym 'Melba'. In 1886, she moved to Europe where she received critical acclaim. She went on to further successes in London and New York.

In the early 20th century she returned to Australia, buying a house near Melbourne and dedicating herself to teaching singing and music and helping to establish the Melbourne Conservatorium. During the First World War, Melba raised money for war charities (almost £100000) and for this she was made into a Dame.

Margaret Court (1942 -)

Born in New South Wales in 1942, Margaret Court is our all-time female tennis great. Between 1960 and 1977, Court won an amazing 24 Grand Slam titles and, an even more amazing, 192 career titles. Court won the Australian Open 11 times, the French Open 5 times, Wimbledon 3 times and the US Open 5 times. She also won 19 Doubles Grand Slam titles and 21 Mixed Doubles Grand Slam titles. In 1970, she completed the Grand Slam, a truly amazing record and one unlikely to ever be beaten. Court is now a Christian Reverend and devotes her time helping the poor and homeless.

Betty Cuthbert (1938 -)

Elizabeth 'Betty' Cuthbert is an Australian sprinter who became a national hero when she won three gold medals in the 100m, 200m and the 4 x 100m relay at the 1956 Melbourne Olympics (as well as another gold in the 400m sprint at the 1964 Tokyo Olympics). Cuthbert has been inducted into both the Australian Sport Hall of Fame and the International Athletics Hall of Fame. She even has a rose named after her.

Sir Charles Kingsford Smith (1897-1935)
Sydney airport is named after this great aviator because, in 1928, Kingsford-Smith made the first Trans-Pacific flight, 83 hours' worth, from America to Australia. He also flew non-stop across Australia and from Australia to New Zealand. In 1935, Kingsford-Smith disappeared while trying to break the record between England and Australia.

Rod Laver (1938 -)
Considered to be the greatest Australian tennis player in history, 'Rocket' Rod, as he is called, was born in Rockhampton, Queensland, in 1938. Laver holds the record for the number of individual titles won (200). He was the world number one player between 1964 and 1970. He has won the Grand Slam twice, in 1962 and 1969. He has won 11 single Grand Slam titles, 9 Grand Slam doubles titles and 4 Grand Slam Mixed Doubles titles, and the list goes on.

Reverend Dr John Flynn (1880-1951)
Given Australia's vast size, proper medical treatment for people living in the Outback was almost non-existent with barely a few doctors to cover the millions of kilometres. Flynn campaigned to have an aerial medical service and in, 1928, an old plane took off from Cloncurry, Queensland, and the Royal Flying Doctor's Service was born. The RFDS now looks after more than 300000 patients and have saved immeasurable numbers of lives.

Sir Edward 'Weary' Dunlop (1907-1993)
An enigmatic figure, Dunlop holds a special reverence for Australians. During the Second World War the Japanese treated Australian, and other Allied, soldiers particularly harshly. The most severe of these was where the soldiers were forced to work on the Burma Death Railway. Dunlop, a thin,

skeleton of a man due to disease and starvation stood up ferociously against his Japanese tormentors to defend the rights of his men.

Albert Jacka VC (1893-1932)
Albert Jacka VC is one of Australia's all-time heroes. Born in 1893 in Victoria, Jacka served as a private at Gallipoli and was the first Australian to receive the Victoria Cross in the First World War. Jacka, single-handedly, after all his mates were killed, held a trench at a place called Courtney's Post overnight. He went on to perform several more acts of bravery and he quickly rose through the ranks. He survived the war and became a businessman and the mayor of St Kilda, in Melbourne. He died in 1932 from wounds he sustained in the war.

Dawn Fraser (1937 -)
One of Australia's all-time greatest swimmers, Fraser won the 100m freestyle at the 1956 Melbourne Olympic Games. She went on to claim the same title in the 1960 and 1964 games. However, she was banned from marching in the opening ceremony in Tokyo after, allegedly, stealing a flag from the Emperor's palace. But 'our' Dawn marched anyway! This led to her being banned from the 1968 games. She would have won it too. The winner was two seconds slower than Fraser's Tokyo time.

Sir Douglas Mawson (1882-1958)
In 1911, Mawson undertook an Antarctic expedition. Mawson went with two others but one fell down a crevasse and the other died from physical exhaustion. In true Aussie style, Mawson went on alone. At 850 kilometres from base camp, Mawson spent 30 days traversing the frozen ice before finally meeting up with other explorers from the expedition.

Dick Smith (1942 -)
One of Australia's most successful entrepreneurs, Richard 'Dick' Harold Smith was born in New South Wales in 1944. Smith started a small car radio business, Dick Smith Electronics, in 1968 which he sold to Woolworths in

1982 for $22 million. Even though he sold the company, there is a chain of stores dotting Australia that still bare his name. Smith has also become famous, not only for his philanthropy and charity work, but also because he created another company in 1999, Dick Smith Foods, in an attempt to stem the tide of increasing foreign ownership of Australian food companies. He also founded the *Australian Geographic* magazine and has become increasingly involved in Australian politics.

Saint Mary Mackillop (1842-1909)
Australia's first, and only, saint, Mary Mackillop began her life in the Outback of South Australia looking after Aboriginal people and orphaned kids. Two women, one in 1961 and one in 1993, both had terminal illnesses and both prayed to Mary. Both were cured. The Vatican considered this to constitute the two miracles needed for sainthood and she was canonised in 2010.

Sir Donald Bradman (1908-2001)
A cricket genius! A maestro! The game's best player! Don Bradman is an absolute national treasure, icon, and hero. There are not enough superlatives to describe a man who averaged 99.94 in Test matches scoring 6996 runs. Bradman is famous for hitting a golf ball with a cricket stump against a corrugated-iron water tank. Bradman became a national ambassador and the only sour note on his cricketing career was the fact that he needed four runs in his last innings to have an overall average of 100. Unfortunately, he was out for a duck (zero). Bradman's significance outside of cricket comes from the fact that he gave so many people hope during the Depression.

Sir Robert Menzies (1894-1978)
Sir Robert Menzies is Australia's longest serving Prime Minister, having been in office continuously from 1939-1941, 1949-1966. Menzies was born in Victoria in 1894 and before entering politics he studied law at the University of Melbourne. Menzies led Australia at the start of the Second World War and it was he who declared war on Germany. Menzies was involved in some of the

biggest Cold War events in Australia such as attempts to ban the Communist Party and the Petrov Affair. Menzies was the presiding Prime Minister when troops were sent into the Korean War and the Vietnam War. He also approved conscription for the latter. At 71 he retired from the role of Prime Minister.

General Sir John Monash (1865-1931)

General Monash was born in Melbourne in 1865 and went on to become a civil engineer before he became Australia's greatest general of the First World War. Monash first served in the ill-fated Gallipoli campaign before going on to fight on the Western Front. Towards the end of the war, Monash was given overall command of the Australian troops (the first time an Australian general was given such a role). Monash planned the attack for the Battle of Amiens, considered one battle that brought an early end to the war. Monash returned to Australia a hero and went on to become a vice-chancellor at the University of Melbourne.

Andrew 'Banjo' Patterson (1864-1941)

Probably the most renowned Australian poet, Patterson's bush verse had become folklore in Australia. The sense of Australian identity, the ability to endure hardship, to thrive in the Outback and our ability to have a good-natured dig at one another is encapsulated in his verses such as *Clancy of the Overflow* and *In Defence of the Bush*. His most famous poem (excerpts of which appear on $10 note) is the *Man from Snowy River*.

The Man from Snowy River (First Verse)

There was movement at the station, for the word had passed around,
That the colt from old Regret had got away,
And had joined the wild bush horses - he was worth a thousand pound,
So all the cracks had gathered to the fray.
All the tried and noted riders from the stations near and far
Had mustered at the homestead overnight,
For the Bushmen love hard riding where the wild bush horses are,
And the stockhorse snuffs the battle with delight.

All Present and Accounted for ...

Aussies Abroad

Aussies have always loved to travel and, as much as we all love our country and it will always be a part of us, some Aussies choose to leave our shores and never come back, or at least for a few years anyway. The Australian Bureau of Statistics (ABS) estimates that, as of 2014, there was more than a million Australians living overseas, almost half of which are living in the United Kingdom (more than 200000 Aussies live in London). The next most popular destination is the United States.

Kylie Minogue

Arguably Australia's most successful female singer, Minogue began her career on the television show, *Neighbours*, before taking her chance and moving to the United Kingdom and giving a singing career a try. Since her first hit, *Locomotion*, Minogue has gone on to have a string of hits such as *Can't Get You Out of My Head* and *Spinning Around*. Minogue performed at the Sydney Olympics and successfully beat breast cancer. Minogue's continued success has earned her the title: 'Pop Princess'.

Clive James

Clive James is an author, essayist, poet and TV personality who has lived in the United Kingdom since 1962. James was born in New South Wales and he eventually went on to study at Cambridge University. After his studies, James started his journalistic career as a TV critic for *The Observer*. His career led him to become a literary critic and prolific author. James has also produced many documentaries and had his own talk shows with series such as *Sunday Night Clive* and *The Clive James Show*.

Andrew Thomas

Andrew 'Andy' Thomas was born in Adelaide in 1951. After his high school studies, Thomas went on to complete his doctorate in mechanical engineering from the University of Adelaide in 1973. Thomas, always fascinated with space, moved to America and applied for American citizenship in 1986 hoping to become part of NASA's astronaut program and, in 1992 he was selected. After a year of training, in 1993 he became qualified to act as a mission specialist on the Space Shuttles. Thomas became the first Australian astronaut in space when he flew on the *Endeavour* mission in 1996. In 1998, he spent 130 days aboard the Russian space station, *Mir*.

Naomi Watts

Although Watts was originally born in England, she moved to Australia with her family when she was 14 (and her maternal grandmother was an Aussie) so we're claiming her. Watts, after an unsuccessful school career, began a career in modelling when she was 18. Watts also entered into acting and went on to have successful roles in Australian soap operas such as *Hey Dad!* And *Home and Away*. She moved to America in 1993 to pursue a film career. After starring in many roles in both film and television, Watts failed to gain true stardom. Her big break came in the physiological thriller, *Mulholland Drive*. Since then she has shot into the international limelight with starring roles in numerous films but primarily in *The Ring* films and the, 2015 release, *Birdman*.

John Pilger

John Pilger is, arguably, one of Australia's best journalists. Born in Bondi in 1939, Pilger attended Sydney Boys' High School, where he started a student newspaper, *The Messenger*, before moving on to work for Australian Consolidated Press. He then worked for the *Sydney Sun* and the *Daily Telegraph* before moving to Britain in 1962. He began working for the *Daily Mirror* and became one of their best foreign correspondents, reporting such events as the Vietnam War. Pilger has gone on to become a heavy critic of the media, particularly in the US, and has written several controversial books.

Geoffrey Robertson

Geoffrey Ronald Robertson QC was born in Sydney and has gone on to become an internationally recognised human rights lawyer, academic, author and television and radio presenter. Robertson studied law in Australia before receiving a Rhodes scholarship at Oxford. Robertson has worked on many high profile cases in both normal legal matters and for human rights cases, such as with Tasmanian Aboriginals trying to retrieve ancestral remains from Britain. His most famous television show is *Geoffrey Robertson's Hypotheticals*, a show which discusses contemporary issues but putting them in hypothetical situations.

Daniel Ricciardo
Ricciardo is currently Australia's premier Formula One driver. Born in Perth in 1989, Ricciardo worked his way through the lower platforms of racing until his predecessor, Mark Webber, retired from F1 and he was elevated to race for Red Bull racing after clocking outstanding times as a test and reserve driver. Ricciardo's first season in an F1 car resulted in him finishing third in the overall driver's standings. Future seasons look promising for this young Aussie.

Rupert Murdoch
One of the world's biggest media moguls, Keith Rupert Murdoch bought his first newspaper, *the Age* in Adelaide in 1953. Murdoch then went on to buy newspapers all across the country. He established the Australian newspaper and this continues to be one of the biggest selling papers. With this success he moved on to buying the *News of the World*, *The Sun* and *The Times*. In 1985, he took up US citizenship, but he is still an Aussie deep down. In the US he created News Corp and 20th Century Fox, building an empire that makes his net worth around $15 billion.

Germaine Greer
Arguably, one of Australia's more controversial women, Germaine Greer was born in Melbourne in 1939. Greer is an Australian academic and writer who is considered one of the strongest and most outspoken voices of feminism in the 20th Century. Her best-selling book, *The Female Eunuch*, released in 1970 has caused, and continues to cause, both admiration and derision. Her ideas on

feminism are more about women finding their own voice and identity rather than finding 'equality' with men.

Andrew Bogut

Andrew Bogut is a 7-foot tall Australian basketball player who has gone on to be highly successful in the NBA, playing with the Milwaukee Bucks and then the Golden State Warriors. When Bogut was drafted by the Bucks he was the number one draft pick, the first Australian to have achieved this honour. Bogut has represented Australia at three Olympic Games and his efforts in the NBA have led many other Aussies to follow in his footsteps.

Australians We Stole From New Zealand

Kiwi author Rosemary Hepozden claims that we Aussies are short of heroes and that we boldly steal them. And she'd be right, but they came to live here so what can we do! Here are a few of the best...

Nancy Wake

Wake worked for the French resistance and she once had a 5 million franc price put on her head by the Gestapo. Named the 'White Mouse' by the Gestapo, Wake, whilst she was born in New Zealand, did move to Australia in 1914. She went to high school in Australia before journeying to London and getting involved in the war. After the war she ran for parliament twice, in Australia, in 1949 and 1966 but was unsuccessful. After that she retired in Port Macquarie, in Australia.

Phar Lap

See *Important Events in Australian History* to see how Aussie he is.

Keith Urban

Australia's hottest, multi-platinum, country artist. Urban was born in New Zealand, but he moved to Caboolture in Queensland when he was aged two. He took up guitar lessons and appeared on Australian shows like *New Faces*.

He went on to appear on Australian country music shows and was awarded a Golden Guitar at the Tamworth Country Music Festival, in Australia. He first signed with the Australian company, EMI, and he has worked with great Australian acts like Slim Dusty and INXS. He is currently married to Australian actress, Nicole Kidman.

Split Enz/Crowded House

Just before they toured Australia in 1973, Split Ends changed the name of the band to 'Split Enz' to make sure the 'NZ' part was known. So, we'll give New Zealand Split Enz but once Neil Finn split the band and founded Crowded House they became Australian. See the section on *Australia's Greatest Bands*.

Russell Crowe

Crowe, who has become one of the biggest movie stars in the world with his roles in movies such as *Gladiator* and *Les Misérables*, was born in the New Zealand capitol, Wellington. True, he went to Auckland Grammar School but he was also educated at Sydney Boys' High School. After his schooling, Crowe returned to Australia at the age of 21 and has lived here ever since. Crowe starred in several Australian soaps but his breakthrough role was in the Australian film, *Romper Stomper*.

Pavlova

According to the Oxford English Dictionary, the 'pav' was introduced to the world in Davis Dainty Dishes, published in 1927 by Kiwi Company Davis Gelatine.

(Ok, we'll give the Kiwis the pav!)

Imported Aussies

We pride ourselves on being multicultural and the idea of a fair go, that anyone who comes to Australia, no matter who they are or what their background, can achieve great things in life. So, we have bred many of our own success stories and heroes but we have also imported a few as well (not just Kiwis!). Their successes just go to show anyone can be an Aussie.

Richard Pratt
Originally from Poland, Pratt moved to the Victorian country town of Shepparton in 1938. Pratt spent time in both London and New York and had some success as an actor. In 1969, he returned home to take over one of Australia's biggest packaging companies, Visy. Pratt was a tremendous philanthropist. He was estimated to be worth $5 billion at the time of his death in April 2009.

Harry Triguboff
Developer of the famous Meriton apartments, Triguboff is of Russian heritage (his family having to flee Stalinist Russia) and, over his life, he has worked as a milkman, a taxi driver and a real estate agent. He bought a block of land in Sydney, developed 8 apartments and he was on his way. His net worth is estimated to be around $4 billion.

Frank Lowy
After spending some of his childhood in detention camps in Cyprus and Palestine, Lowy came to Australia in 1952. By 1959, he had built his first shopping centre. As of 2010, his Westfield shopping centre empire gave him an estimated worth of more than $5 billion. Australia's richest man is also a survivor of Nazi concentration camps.

The Bee Gees
Whilst they only lived in Australia for a few shorts years, after moving from Manchester to Redcliffe, Qld, then back to the United Kingdom again, the disco kings with hits such as *Staying Alive* and *Saturday Night Fever*, have become international superstars and icons of the 1970s. Even if they did move back to England we still consider them to be Aussies.

Victor Chang

Born in China in 1936, Victor Chang would go on to become one of Australia's greatest surgeons. While working at Sydney's St Vincent's Hospital, Chang pioneered the artificial heart valve and heart transplant operations. Between 1984 and 1990, Chang and his team performed more than 200 transplant operations with a 90% success rate. In an unceremonious ending, Chang was shot, in 1991, by two Malaysian men in a failed extortion attempt.

Anh Do

Born in 1977, Do escaped communist Vietnam in 1980. He, and his family, travelled in a leaky fishing boat and were attacked by pirates, twice, before being picked up by a German merchant ship. Do has gone on to become a recognised Australian author (of the best-selling *The Happiest Refugee*), comedian and actor.

Tan Le

Born in Vietnam in 1977, Le and her family escaped communist Vietnam in 1982. Le has gone on to become one of Australia's greatest telecommunication entrepreneurs and created such things as *emotive.com*. In 1998 she was voted *Young Australian of the Year* and she is considered to be one of Australia's Top 30 Most Successful women.

Les Murray

Les Murray has become the face of football (soccer) in Australia due to his work broadcasting the game on the multicultural television channel, the Special Broadcasting Service (SBS). Originally born in Budapest, Hungary. His family migrated to Australia in 1957. Murray has played a dramatic role in the rise and prominence of soccer in Australia since as far back as the 1980s.

Mel Gibson

Mel Gibson is one of the biggest names in acting today with a string of hit films. Mel is considered to be an Aussie but he was actually born in New York in 1956. His parents migrated to Sydney when he was 12 and Gibson went on to study at the prestigious National Institute of Dramatic Art (NIDA). Gibson's big break came in the *Mad Max* films and then in the film *Gallipoli*.

Nicole Kidman

Internationally acclaimed, Australian actress, Nicole Kidman was actually born in Honolulu, Hawaii in 1967. Her parents were on educational visas at the time so, even though she was born to Australian parents but on US territory, she has both Australian and US citizenship. Her first major film was the 1989 thriller, *Dead Calm*, and she has since gone on to star in a dozens of successful films.

Hugo Weaving

One of Australia's most versatile actors, Weaving has gained increased international prominence due to his roles as Mr Smith in the *Matrix* movies and as Lord Elrond in *The Lord of the Rings*. Weaving was born in Nigeria in 1960. After moving around the world with his parents, he finally settled with them in Sydney in 1976.

Judy Cassab

Judy Cassab is an Australian painter who is the only woman to win the Archibald Prize (the highest award for portraits in the country) twice in 1960 and 1967. Cassab is of Hungarian background and was born in Vienna in 1920. Her parents, after being put in a Nazi forced labour camp, migrated to Australia in 1950.

Sir Gustav Nosel

Sir Gustav Nosel is a world-renowned Australian research biologist who has become famous for his work with immunisation and antibody research. Nosel was born in Vienna in 1931. His family, given their grandparents were Jewish, decided to leave Austria in 1939 after it was annexed by Hitler and the Nazis. He arrived in Australia speaking no English but still managed to learn and finish Dux of St Aloysius' College. He was knighted for his immunology work in 1977, listed as an *Australian Living Treasure* in 1997 and was named the *Australian of the Year* in 2000.

Dr Karl Kruszelnicki

Dr Karl, as he is known to Australian audiences, is a popular scientist on Australian television. Kruszelnicki, of Polish parents, was born in Helsingborg, Sweden, after his father and mother had survived the Holocaust and decided to flee Europe. Dr Karl arrived in Australia with his parents at the age of 2, spending time in a refugee camp before his family moved to Wollongong. Kruszelnicki was awarded the *Father of the Year* in 2003. In 2012, he was named as a *National Living Treasure* and he was voted in *Reader's Digest* as the ninth most trusted Australian.

Famous Indigenous Australians

David Unaipon (1872-1967)

Featured on the Australian $50 bill, Unaipon was an Ngarrindjeri man who worked as a preacher, inventor and writer. Unaipon invented mechanical shearing machines and other mechanical devices. He also had ideas for helicopters prior to the First World War. Unaipon was the first Aboriginal author to be published, writing articles on everything mechanical to Aboriginal legends and Aboriginal rights. He also wrote a book of traditional Aboriginal stories, entitled, *Myths and Legends of Aboriginal Australians*. Unaipon was, undoubtedly, one of the first pioneers of Aboriginal activism.

Adam Goodes (1980 -)

Adam Goodes is an Australian Rules Football player with the Sydney Swans team. He is a dual Brownlow Medallist (the highest individual award in the game), dual premiership winner and four-time All-Australian representative. He was also voted *Australian of the Year* in 2014. Goodes' legacy, apart from his exploits on the footy field, will be his tireless campaigning against racism, having been subject to such things himself.

Lionel Rose (1948-2011)
A Japanese boxer, Fighting Harada, was unbeaten between 1963 and 1968 in the bantamweight division. A quiet country boy from Melbourne, Lionel Rose, travelled to Tokyo and fought a hard fifteen rounds, winning on a judges' decision. Rose became the first Aboriginal to win a world title in any sport.

Mandaway Yunupingu (1956-2013)
Yunupingu was a well-known educator and musician, fronting the band, Yothu Yindi. The band had the first charting hit from an Aboriginal band, *Treaty*. Yunupingu was also a community activist and became principal of the Yirrkala Community School. He was also part of the Yolgnu Action Group that advocated a mix of Aboriginal tradition teachings and modern Western methods. Yunupingu was voted *Australian of the Year* in 1992.

Evonne Goolagong Cawley (1951 -)
Cawley is a Wiradjuri woman who achieved fame as a worldwide tennis star in the late 1970s and early 1980s. A number one ranked player, Cawley won 14 Grand Slam titles (four Australian Opens, two Wimbledon Championships, and one French Open, as well as six women's Doubles titles and one Mixed Doubles title. Born in country New South Wales, Cawley overcame racial barriers to learn to play tennis. She continues to work as a Sports Ambassador for Aboriginal people and runs development camps to help more Aboriginal students get into the game. She was voted *Australian of the Year* in 1972, and, in 1988, was inducted to the International Tennis Hall of Fame.

Cathy Freeman (1973 -)
A truly great sprinter. (See **the Five Greatest Moments in Australian Sport** for more info. See page 144).

Jessica Mauboy (1989 -)
Mauboy is an R & B/ pop singer who was discovered when she was runner-up on talent show, *Australian Idol*, in 2006. Since then she has gone on to sell

millions of albums and has forged a successful acting career, appearing in such films as *The Sapphires* (the story of four Aboriginal girls who perform for the troops in Vietnam). She has donated money to the Children's Hospital and performed free to raise money for the Royal Flying Doctor's Service as well as promoting Aboriginal schools and learning.

Charles Perkins (1936-2000)
In the late 1960s, a well-educated Aboriginal man, Charles Perkins, led a series of Freedom Rides (based on similar events which occurred in the United States) through country New South Wales to highlight injustices against Indigenous people. Perkins was the first Indigenous person to graduate from university and he also played soccer for Everton in the United Kingdom.

Albert Namatjira (1902- 1959)
Born in 1902 in Alice Springs, Albert Namatjira is one of Australia's great artists. An Arrente man, he was a pioneer of Indigenous Australian painting, famous for his watercolours of the desert and the Outback. In 1957 he was the first Aboriginal Australian to be granted full Australian citizenship, allowing him the right to vote, to build a house and to buy alcohol (all things Aboriginal people were not allowed to do). He also went on to win the Archibald Prize. However, citizenship rights brought about another set of problems. In Aboriginal culture, a person is expected to share everything they have with their people. This led to Namatjira losing most of his money and being imprisoned for supplying alcohol to his people (when the law prohibited this). Namatjira died soon afterwards.

Archie Roach (1956 -)
Born in 1956 in country Victoria, Archie Roach has gone on to become a highly successful and acclaimed musician and songwriter. Despite having an unpleasant childhood, being taken away from his parents and family, Roach's powerful music has become an outlet for Indigenous issues, particularly his song about the Stolen Generations called *They Took the Children Away*. In his

own words, 'My lyrics draw attention to the hardship and humiliation suffered by many Indigenous Australians.' This song has also achieved an *International Human Rights* award. Roach now spends his time recording and working with troubled Aboriginal youth.

Lt Reginald Saunders (1920-1990)
Born in Victoria, Reginald Saunders was the first Aboriginal serviceman to be commissioned as an officer in the Australian Army. Saunders served with distinction in the Second World War, first fighting in Greece, Crete and then in New Guinea. He then went on to fight in Korea, particularly at the famous Battle of Kapyong.

David Gulpilil (1953 -)
Gulpilil is a renowned Aboriginal dancer and actor. Born in Arnhem Land in the Northern Territory in 1953, Gulpilil's extraordinary skills gained him his first role in the film, *Walkabout*. Gulpilil's talents led him to travel the world and meet such famous people as John Lennon, Bob Marley, Muhammad Ali and Bruce Lee. In 2014, Gulpilil won a Best Actor award at the Cannes Film Festival for his role in the film, *Charlie's Country*, amongst many other awards. He has starred in dozens of films and now spends much of his time mentoring young Aboriginals and campaigning for Aboriginal Land Rights and for compensation for The Stolen Generations.

Local Knowledge: Aussie Bands that we love, but the world may not have necessarily heard of

AC/DC
Known as 'Acca Dacca' to Aussies, AC/DC is the most famous of Australian bands and is one Aussie band that have made it on the worldwide stage. Formed in 1973, they have had many huge hits and they are one of the best-selling bands of all time, selling more than 200 million albums. Their biggest album, *Back in Black*, is still in the top ten highest selling albums of

all time. AC/DC was originally fronted by Bon Scott but he tragically died from complications with alcohol. Now with front man, Brian Johnson, AC/DC is also characterised by the school boy uniforms of lead guitarist, Angus Young. Other 'Acca Dacca' hits include *Highway to Hell*, *Thunderstruck* and *High Voltage*.

INXS

INXS began life in Sydney in 1977 when the three Farriss brothers, Andrew, John and Tim, joined with charismatic and, eventual, pure rock star, Michael Hutchence as well as Kirk Pengilly and Garry Beers. Their first number one single in the US, and the song that meant they hit the big time, was *Original Sin*. Their albums *Listen Like Thieves* and *Kick* further cemented their place as international superstars, with the band having sold over 40 million albums worldwide. The original band ended in 1997 when Michael Hutchence was found dead in his hotel room in 1997. Other INXS hits include *Never Tear Us Apart*, *Need You Tonight* and *Suicide Blonde*.

Midnight Oil

Probably Australia's most political band and, apart from their strong political views, they are probably best characterised by their bald-headed, interesting dancing style, lead singer, Peter Garrett. Midnight Oil, or 'the Oils', were formed in Canberra in 1976. The key themes that the Oils wanted to bring attention to Aussie audiences was Indigenous rights (with songs like *Beds Are Burning*), anti-nuclear/anti US sentiment (with songs like *Power and the Passion*) and environmentalism (with songs like *Blue Sky Mining*). *Diesel and Dust* is Midnight Oil's biggest selling album both within Australia and internationally. Interestingly, the lead singer, Peter Garrett went on to become the Environment Minister for the Gillard Labor government.

Cold Chisel

Cold Chisel, or simply 'Chisel', are probably the biggest band in Australia to not have achieved international success. Chisel are responsible for a series of

Aussie classics such as *Flame Trees, Cheap Wine, When the War is Over* and *Khe Sanh*. Originally formed in Adelaide in 1973, Cold Chisel is fronted by the enigmatic Jimmy Barnes and the soulful, Ian Moss. Whilst Don Walker wrote many of Chisel's songs, it has been a true team effort and Chisel are the only Aussie rock band to have had successful songs written by all members of the band. Chisel are the classic Australian pub rock band and many of their songs have become working-class anthems.

The Angels
Another band formed in Adelaide, The Angels began life in 1974. Led by front man Doc Neeson, they are another quintessential Aussie pub rock band. The most renowned Angel's song has to be *Am I Ever Gonna See Your Face Again?* When sung in pubs around the country the response to the chorus is 'No Way, Get F#cked, F#@k off!' Their classic songs also include *No Secrets* and *Take A Long Line*. Famous bands such as Pearl Jam, Guns and Roses and Nirvana have cited the Angels as influencing their own music.

Hunters and Collectors
Originally from Melbourne, and formed in 1981, Hunters and Collectors have been responsible for such classic Aussie songs as *Throw Your Arms Around Me, When The River Runs Dry* and *Holy Grail*. Hunters and Collectors have an eclectic sound and, as such, have cemented their place as one of Australia's best live acts.

Powderfinger
Powderfinger is one of the biggest bands to come out of Brisbane. Formed in 1989 and led by Bernard Fanning, Powderfinger had several top-selling albums, such as *Odyssey Number Five*, and produced classic Aussie songs such as *These Days* and *My Happiness*.

Powderfinger have been prominent in helping raise funds for breast cancer research and to help raise awareness about the gap between the life expectancies and education for Indigenous and non-Indigenous peoples. They also organised concerts to fundraise for disaster relief. They called it quits in 2010.

Crowded House

While there is debate over whether Crowded House are Kiwis or Aussies, Crowded House were formed in Melbourne in 1985 and so we're claiming them! Added to this, two of the first three founding members, Paul Hester and Nick Seymour are Aussies, so we're doubly claiming them! Crowded House made it big internationally receiving the MTV Music Award for *Best New Artist* in 1987 as well as being named *International Group of the Year* at the 1994 Brit Awards. Driving force Neil Finn (a Kiwi, taken!) penned such classics as *Don't Dream It's Over*, *Weather With You* and *Distant Sun* and over 100,000 fans packed the Sydney Opera House for their final concert in 1996.

The Easybeats

Formed in Sydney in 1964, the Easybeats were Australia's answer to the Beatles. They were the first Australian act to have an international hit with *Friday on My Mind* (rated at the turn of the millennium as the greatest song ever written by an Australian band). Led by enigmatic lead singer, Stevie Wright, the band was a mixture of migrants, having been formed in the Villawood Migrant Hostel (now known as the Villawood Detention Centre). The Easybeats also had such hits as *She's So Fine*, *I'll Make You Happy* and *Good Times*. The group disbanded in 1969 when different members decided to pursue their own individual careers.

Paul Kelly

While Paul Kelly himself, is not a band, Kelly has been involved with bands such as *The Dots*, *The Coloured Girls* and *The Messengers* and his music covers several genres such as folk, rock and country. Kelly was born in Adelaide before he moved to Melbourne in 1976 and then to Sydney and then back to Melbourne. Kelly has written many Australian classics such as *To Her Door*, *Dumb Things* and *How to Make Gravy*. Kelly is considered by many to be the finest songwriter in Australia.

Honorary Mentions:
Little River Band, Air Supply, The Saints, Silverchair, Wolfmother, The
Living End.

Local Knowledge: Top 20 Aussie Essential Listening
The best Australian songs of all time are always a hotly debated topic, in fact,
an Australia Day tradition is the Triple J Hottest 100. The following selection,
therefore, aims to list the best songs to give the foreign visitor an idea about
Australia, Aussies and Aussie culture – these are twenty classic songs that,
when they come on the radio or jukebox every Aussie knows the words and will
sing-a-long.

1. *Down Under* – Men At Work
2. *Sounds of Then* – Ganggajang
3. *It's a Long Way to the Top* – AC/DC
4. *Khe Sanh* – Cold Chisel
5. *Never Tear Us Apart* – INXS
6. *To Her Door* – Paul Kelly
7. *Flame Trees* – Cold Chisel
8. *Great Southern Land* – Icehouse
9. *Throw Your Arms Around Me* – Hunters and Collectors
10. *Solid Rock* – Goanna Power
11. *Beds are Burning* – Midnight Oil
12. *Island Home* – Christine Anu or Warumpi band
13. *Treaty* – Yothu Yindi
14. *True Blue* – John Williamson
15. *You're the Voice* – John Farnham
16. *Still Call Australia Home* – Peter Allen
17. *Working Class Man* – Jimmy Barnes
18. *Pub With No Beer* – Slim Dusty
19. *Reckless* – Australian Crawl
20. *Am I Ever Gonna See Your Face Again?* – The Angels

Ten Great Australia Films

As with many top 10s, everybody has their own version. Many Aussies would disagree with the following however, the list is formed on the basis for the best 10 films for the overseas visitor to gain the best understanding of Aussie lifestyle and culture, not the best films on cinematic merit.

Gallipoli (1981)

Gallipoli is the story of Frank and Archie, two young Aussie men who join the Australian Imperial Force (AIF) and head to Egypt and then to the foreign shores of Turkey to fight for their country. Directed by Peter Weir, *Gallipoli* gives a great portrayal of life in Australia in the early 20th century but also the loss of innocence of a generation of Australian youth during the campaign, which is considered to be the birth of the modern Australian nation.

The Castle (1997)

When watching the 1997 film, *The Castle*, the foreign visitor would be forgiven for needing to use a slang translator. The movie is the story of the Kerrigan family who live on the outskirts of Melbourne and their house is threatened by a compulsory acquisition of their home by developers. *The Castle* is the true Aussie Battler story. The movie has also created such one liners which have entered use in everyday Australian such as 'how's the serenity?' and 'tell him he's dreaming!' Interestingly, when the film was released in America many Aussie words needed to be changed. Most Aussies would agree that this film is the one Australian film that best represents who we are as a nation.

Crocodile Dundee (1986)

Undoubtedly the one film that really took Aussie culture to the world, *Crocodile Dundee*, is the story of Outback crocodile hunter, Mick Dundee. A journalist from New York comes across the story of Dundee and travels to his hometown of Walkabout Creek to see what the crocodile man is all about. The film contains excellent cinematography of the Outback but also gives the viewer a good understanding of what Aussies in the Outback are all about. Dundee travels to

New York, his time there a tongue-in-cheek example of some Australians lack of knowledge about the rest of the world. Many Australians wouldn't be aware that there are, in fact, two versions of the film, the second version having much of the Australian slang replaced for international audiences.

Breaker Morant (1980)
Harry 'Breaker' Morant was an Australian (although he was originally British) soldier who was executed for the murder of civilians while fighting in the Boer War in South Africa in 1902. The story of Breaker Morant contains traditional ideas of mateship, the bush and the laid back attitude. However, the Breaker Morant story is one of the most hotly debated historical topics in Australia. Was he a hero or a villain?

Mad Max (1979)
All four *Mad Max* films has received international acclaim, but to get an idea of Australia in the late 1970s there really is only the first film to watch as the sequels take place in a post-apocalyptic Australia. Max Rockatansky (Mel Gibson) is a policeman in a world facing an energy crisis. The Acolytes motorcycle gang runs wild on the streets, terrorising the people and taking whatever they please. After the gang murders his wife and child, Max sets out in his black pursuit vehicle (a highly-charged Ford) and systematically hunts down each gang member one by one. *Mad Max* was, for a time, the most profitable Aussie film.

The Adventures of Priscilla: Queen of the Desert (1994)
An unlikely Aussie hit, Priscilla is the story of two drag queens and a transsexual woman who travel across the Simpson Desert meeting various, and different, individuals along the way. Priscilla not only has great cinematic views of the Outback but gives a little bit of an insight into the types of characters you might come across in the central parts of Australia. Priscilla opened up Australian cinema to the world and foreigners began to realise the quirky nature of the Aussie sense of humour. The costumes from Priscilla were even

used in the Sydney 2000 Olympics opening ceremony to showcase Australian popular culture.

Rabbit Proof Fence (2002)
Rabbit Proof Fence follows the story of three young Aboriginal girls, Molly, Gracie and Daisy, who are forcibly removed from their mothers and sent to the Moore River Native Settlement to be taught the 'civilised' ways of the white population. The girls escape, led by Molly, and follow the nine-week journey of 2400 kilometres (1500 miles) as they walk along the rabbit fence to get back to their hometown of Jigalong, all the while being hunted by the authorities.

Released in 2002, *Rabbit Proof Fence* brought the ideas of the Stolen Generations to a wider Australian audience and certainly played a role in the Reconciliation movements that came in the subsequent years.

The Man from Snowy River (1982)
If any foreign visitor were to watch a film to get an idea about Australian identity then *The Man from Snowy River* would be the one. The 1982 film, based on the classic poem by Banjo Patterson, follows the story of Jim, a young stock hand who is trying to earn the respect of the fellow stockmen. It is also the love story of Jim and Jessica. The film and the poem, climaxes with the attempt to capture the untameable wild horse (a brumby).

Two Hands (1999)
Two Hands is a 1999 Aussie crime film. Set in Sydney, the story follows the lives of the film's main character, Jimmy (Heath Ledger), who is in debt to local King's Cross gangsters, and Jimmy's love interest, Alex (Rose Byrne). *Two Hands* highlights the seedier underside of Sydney at the turn of the millennium and it also showcases many of the city's famous sites.

Muriel's Wedding (1994)
The film that launched Toni Collette's career, *Muriel's Wedding* takes place in the made-up town of Porpoise Spit. A classic Aussie comedy, it revolves

around the socially awkward ugly duckling, Muriel, and her attempts to get out of her dead-end town and move to the big smoke, Sydney. Muriel does this, only to find out that her dream life was not all that she expected. *Muriel's Wedding* is a tongue-in-cheek look at the sometimes-darker side of suburban Australia.

Chapter Four:

Who's that in Your Wallet?

Aussie Money and its Meaning

The original Australian economy was rum and a barter system.

Early coins and notes were a mixture of English and Spanish coins. Governor Macquarie, not wanting the Spanish coins back on the ships, ordered the centres of the Spanish coins pressed out. The coins with the holes became 'holeys' and the centres called 'dumps'. These coins were pressed with a New South Wales stamp in 1813, the holey pressed with 'five shillings' and the dumps pressed with 'fifteen pence'.

In 1817, the Bank of New South Wales was created and the first banknotes in Australia were issued, including five shillings, ten shillings, one pound and five pounds. Paper tokens were also created for one and two shillings and one and two shillings and sixpence.

In 1913 the first series of Australian notes was issued, based on the old British system of 12 pence to a shilling, 20 shillings to a pound. Slang terms for these amounts still continue to be used in Australian vernacular today such as 'quid' and 'two bob' (twenty cents).

On Valentine's Day, 1966, we changed to the decimal system. Many names, such as 'austral', 'merino' and 'royals', were thrown around as potential candidates but sanity prevailed and 'dollars and cents' were accepted. The reason for the change was two-fold. Firstly, to bring it into line with more 'modern' currencies such as that in the US and to create a series of coins and notes that was more Australian in design.

In order to help the transition, the Australian government developed a song for people to remember (with the same tune as a famous Australian ballad, *Click Goes the Shears*):

> *In come the dollars, in come the cents,*
> *To replace the pounds and shillings and the pence.*
> *Be prepared for the changes when the coins begin to mix,*
> *On the 14th of February, 1966.*

The lasting legacy of the British when it comes to our money is the fact that you will find the Queen on one side of our coins and, if you look closely, you will notice that the portrait of the queen changes with the age of the coin.

Australia, having had problems with counterfeiting over the years, was the first country in the world to have a complete set of notes made from plastic (polymer). As an extra bonus, the polymer notes last up to four times longer than the traditional paper note.

Five Cents	The 5 cent coin has an echidna, sometimes called a spiny anteater, it is one of two monotremes (egg-laying mammals).
Ten Cents	The 10 cent coin features a dancing male lyrebird.
Twenty Cents	The 20 cent coin carries a platypus, the world's other monotreme.
Fifty Cents	The 50 cent coin has Australia's coat of arms on the main side.
$1 coin	The $1 coin, which replaced the $1 note in 1984, has five kangaroos in various poses. The $1 coin also changes to celebrate various important Australian and world events.
$2 coin	The $2 coin, replacing the $2 note in 1988, has a portrait of an Aboriginal tribal elder with the Southern Cross and native trees in the background.
$5	The $5 note features Her Majesty Queen Elizabeth II and Parliament House in Canberra.
$10	The $10 note has famous Australian poets, 'Banjo' Paterson and Dame Mary Gilmore. The note has examples of each poets work on it!
$20	The $20 note has Reverend John Flynn on one side and Mary Reibey on the other. Reibey came to Australia in 1792 as a convict but after being granted her freedom, she went on to become a successful shipping magnate and philanthropist.
$50	The $50 note has Aboriginal writer and inventor David Unaipon on one side and the first female elected to Parliament, Edith Cowan, on the other.
$100	The $100 note features world-renowned soprano Dame Nellie Melba (1861–1931), and the distinguished soldier, engineer and administrator General Sir John Monash (1865–1931).

Local Knowledge: Clean Up Australia Day

Every year hundreds of thousands of Aussie get out on *Clean Up Australia Day* to help clean up our country. *Clean Up Australia Day* was the brainchild of Ian Kiernan and Kim McKay. Started in 1990, *Clean Up Australia Day* is held on the first Sunday of March each year. 2015 marks the 25th anniversary of the event. In 2014, there were more than half a million volunteers who cleaned up more than 15 tonnes of rubbish. Since its inception, *Clean Up Australia Day* has collected almost 300000 tonnes of rubbish.

Chapter Five:

How to Be Mistaken
for an Aussie

Understanding What Aussies Are All About

In order to be mistaken for an Aussie you must first understand those things by which us Aussies define ourselves and the role that these traditions play in how we conduct our everyday lives. A few things to keep in mind:

- *You have to look out for your mates* - There is nothing more important than being there for your mates, especially when they are down and out and need your help.
- *Always back the battler* - Aussies always back the underdog or the person who has their back against the wall, the battler.
- *No worries* – No matter what happens, no matter how bad things get, everything is 'no worries'.
- *Be a larrikin* – Never, ever, take yourself or life too seriously.

The Anzac Tradition

Many people define their national identity by the moment their nation was born; Aussies tend not to define themselves by Federation (the actual moment our nation was born) but with the 'birth' of our nation with our first battle in the First World War.

Australians had fought in previous wars, such as the Boer War in South Africa, but only ever as colonial regiments. The first war where Aussies fought as a unified force was in the First World War. Hundreds of thousands of Australians answered the Mother Country's (Britain) calls for help.

The Australians were first sent to Egypt to train and, during this time, the name ANZAC (Australia New Zealand Army Corp) was given to the Australian and New Zealander troops. The origins of the word are obscure but the general idea is that a British clerk, in order to make his job easier, formed the acronym.

Most of the first soldiers expected to be sent to the Western Front in France but, given Turkey's entrance into the war on the side of Germany, the first soldiers were sent to a peninsula in Turkey the Australians called 'Gallipoli'.

At 4:30 in the morning the Australians and Kiwis, landed at a beach which is now called ANZAC Cove. Under heavy fire, they managed to clamber onto the beach and up the cliffs and stake a foothold in Turkey.

With heavy losses on both sides, the Gallipoli campaign was a failure but out of it came many things that make up the modern day Australian and how we perceive the world.

The first of these is mateship. This is a key element to the Australian identity; it's all about sticking by your mates no matter what.

The second is the larrikin, or joker, attitude. While serious about what we do in life, Australians try not to take themselves too seriously and try to find a joke in everything.

The last is a courage and endurance. The Diggers had to endure the worst conditions at Gallipoli such as heat, lice and dysentery. Modern Aussies (although hopefully dysentery is not such a problem anymore!) pride themselves on their ability to get through things.

How to Sound Like an Aussie

The Australian accent has developed out of the two hundred years of European settlement. Given a whole bunch of different accented English speakers were on the First Fleet it is no surprise that we have developed an accent all of our own. Aussies, depending on which state you are in; either speak extremely quickly or extremely slowly. We tend to run our words together or don't finish them at all. And we often don't bother finishing our sentences. Some Australians will speak clearly, others will sound like they are actually speaking through their nose.

Really, to speak like an Aussie, all you need to do is take normal, full English words and cut them off and replace the end with an 'o'. For example, afternoon becomes 'arvo', service station becomes 'servo' and so on. Or for common words take the word and add 'y' or 'ie' to the end. Breakfast – Brekkie.

Australian English is full of colourful slang, both rhyming and normal, and speaking to an Aussie (particularly someone from the country or from the older generations) can be akin to talking to someone in another language.

The origins of the Australian 'drawl' are somewhat obscure – but it is generally agreed that it comes from our convict heritage and, because of the 'criminal' heritage; many prisoner words worked their way into the Australian language. Given the fact that much of the convicts either came from the East End of London, Scotland and Ireland we seem to have adopted various nuances from all of them.

How to Talk Like an Aussie

In Australia your name is not always your name and an Australian may take on several nicknames, the most common being a change in your surname. Just like long words that we couldn't be bothered to finish, surnames are often shortened and the last syllable replaced with an 'o'. For example, a man called David Jackson, will become 'Davo' or 'Jacko.'

The other option for a nickname from a surname is to replace the last syllable with an 'ie' or a 'y'. For example, Foster becomes Fozzie or Fozzy.

The height of the laziness of the Australian language comes to the fore with words like thingo, dooverlackie, whadjamacallit, whatsit, thingamy, all used to refer to a non-specific item when we can't remember its name.

If one Australian said to another, 'hand me the dooverlackie for the thingo', the other Australian would know exactly what the first Australian was referring to!

Many Australians, particularly, older women and gentlemen will use words such as 'darl/ darling', 'love', 'sweetie' in everyday speech. Many travellers may feel a little awkward at this but it is a term of affection and the person does not mean any harm.

Other confusing aspects of Aussie speech include:

- *Yeah, Nah* – Aussies will often respond to a question by saying, 'yeah, nah.' While you might think the person is saying yes, they actually mean 'no'.
- *But* – Aussies will often finish their sentence with the word 'but'. For example, 'I won't arrive until seven, but…' Those who have learnt the

Queen's English, like the Poms, would then expect one to finish the sentence but, no, the sentence is complete.

- Many Australians, particularly older ones, still use a lot of the rhyming slang that originated in Britain. Rhyming slang came about from the prisoners (soon to be convicts) trying to speak without the local constabulary being able to understand what they are saying. These are still heavily used in England and anyone watching Guy Ritchie's films like *Snatch* and *Lock, Stock and Two Smoking Barrels* would understand the difficulty in rhyming slang for the uninitiated.

Some examples of rhyming slang still in use in Australia include:

Dog's eye – Meat pie.

Skyrocket – Pocket.

Butcher's hook – To take a look.

Captain Cook – Also, to take a look.

Dead Horse – Tomato sauce.

Horse and Cart – To fart.

Frog and Toad – Road.

Dog and Bone – Phone.

Joe Blake – Snake.

Pat Malone – On one's own.

Noah's Ark – Shark.

Trouble and Strife – Wife.

Having a Barry Crocker – having a shocker (or bad time).

Porky Pies – Lies (sometimes shortened to Porkies).

Do the Harold Holt – to do the bolt (a slang term for running away or disappearing).

Jatz Crackers – a popular biscuit, 'crackers' rhymes with 'knackers', a slang term for the male parts.

Grundies – undies, rhymes with Reg Grundy, the television producer.

How to Swear Like an Aussie

Have no bones about it, Australians like to swear and, particularly in the country, people, both men and women, will construct entire sentences using only, or mostly, swear words.

The swear word you will hear Australians most use is 'bloody'. Oddly enough, in generations gone by this was considered a swear word, but in modern Australia it is not considered a rude word. However, it did cause controversy when it was used in an Australian tourism advertising campaign where an attractive, bikini clad Aussie girl asked: 'Where the bloody hell are ya'?' Whilst we merely meant 'why are you not here?' the Poms seemed to take great offence to this.

Another curiosity for overseas travellers is how Australians refer to one another, particularly the fact that seemingly insulting terms are used as terms of endearment.

For example, 'garn get stuffed ya' bastard!' Directly translated would be, 'go and fill yourself with something, you child of a non-married couple.' However, you would be wrong – in fact, it means 'yeah, you got me, friend.'

There are several other words that, if you took them literally, you would be somewhat confused but, in fact, are used as affectionate terms.

One example of this is 'wanker'. The direct meaning of the word is someone who masturbates – however, it can be used as both a derogatory term and an affectionate one.

'Ah, get stuffed, ya' wanker.' Translation: 'Leave me alone, mate!'
Or
'Geez, that bloke's a real wanker!' Translation: what a moron.

The other word that has taken on a completely different meaning to the definition in the dictionary is 'bugger'. Now, the direct meaning of the word is sexual relations between two males. However, you will often hear Aussies saying, 'I'm buggered,' or, 'bugger me!' Let's be clear on this, they are not asking you to have said relations with them. These two phrases translate to, 'I am extremely tired' and, 'wow, I can't believe it!'

Another very common Australian phrase that is the cause of much confusion amongst foreigners is, 'this is givin' me the shits.' Directly translated, one would think that, whatever the problem may be, the person has a severe case of diarrhoea. In fact, it merely means that the person is upset.

Aussies also have quite interesting ways of referring to sex that may confuse visitors (or, even worse, get them in to some trouble). When an Australian male or female refers to, 'having a root' or, 'getting a root', they, in fact, mean 'having sex'. As you can imagine, when Americans say they are 'rooting' for their team, we Aussie tend to have a giggle.

Some Aussie Insults...

A few Kangaroos short in the top paddock: someone a bit dim.

A few sandwiches short of a picnic basket: someone a bit dim.

As useful as tits on a bull: bloody useless.

As boring as batshit: rather uninteresting.

Dumb as dogshit: stupid.

As thick as two short planks: someone who is not very bright.

A Glossary of Australian Slang Terms

The entirety of Australian slang would warrant a book all of its own so the following is a brief guide to some of the most common slang terms. It is important to know at least some Aussie slang. Some Australians use very little slang and will be easily understood, while others will construct sentences that are almost all slang terms and can hardly be understood! But, one thing is for sure, all Australians use, at least, some slang.

A

Aerial Ping Pong: Australian Rules football.

Ankle biter: a small child.

Apples, she'll be: it'll be all right.

Argie-Bargie: an argument or confrontation.

B

Bananas: to go 'bananas' or to go crazy.

Battler: someone who works hard but is still struggling to make a living.

Beaut, beauty: something great or fantastic.

Beer Goggles: imaginary goggles that make the opposite sex look more attractive after a few beers.

Beer O'clock: time of the day when beer drinking begins.

Bee's Knees: something that is particularly good.

Big-note oneself: to brag or boast.

Bloody oath!: that couldn't be truer.

Bludger: a lazy person, someone who does very little or lets someone else do everything for them.

Blue: to have a fight, for example, 'he's having a blue with his mate.'

Bogan: a lower class person, generally a beer drinking bludger.

Boofhead: an idiot or someone silly.

Bonzer: Really, really good.

Bottle-o: a liquor shop. The name derives from when a man would come around and collect your bottles in the 50s and 60s.

Buckley's/ Buckley's chance: absolutely no chance of winning. One story goes that Buckley was an escaped convict who, when his mates ran out of food, ate Buckley instead. Hence, no chance.

Budgie smugglers: men's Speedos/ swimming underpants. Something our current Prime Minister, Tony Abbott, is renowned for wearing.

C

Cactus: stuffed or useless. For example, 'the washing machine is cactus.'

Cakehole: your mouth, as in, 'shut your cakehole!'

Cark it: to die or when something ceases to function, for example, 'the washing machine is going to cark it.'

Carry on like a pork chop: to act like an idiot.

Cat burying shit, as busy as a: to be extremely busy.

Cat's piss: as in this tastes like cat's piss, although one must wonder who the first person was to discover this and why?

Charge like a wounded bull: something that is ridiculously expensive.

Cheap as chips: an excellent price.

Chockers: very full.

Chook: a chicken.

Chrissie: Christmas.

Chuck a sickie: take the day off sick from work even when you're perfectly healthy.

Chunder: vomit

Clanger: a big mistake.

Come a gutser: to have a bad accident.

Corker: something excellent.

Coldie: a cold beer.

Crickey!: excitement of disbelief, made internationally famous by the late Steve Irwin.

Crook: to be sick or something that is poorly made.

Cut snake, mad as a: to be very, very angry.

D

Dag: an idiot, or goofy person.

Daks: trousers.

Deadset: the absolute truth.

Derro: shortened version of derelict, which is, a tramp or homeless person.

Dill: an idiot.

Dinkum, fair dinkum: the truth. Also, often used as a question – 'is he fair dinkum?'

Dinky-di: the real thing.

Dipstick/ Dipshit: a loser or idiot.

Dob (somebody) in: to tell on someone, someone who 'dobs' is referred to as a 'dobber'.

Dollop: a small portion.

Donkey's/ Donkey's years: having not seen someone or done something in a long time.

Drongo: an idiot or very stupid person.

Dummy, spit the: to get extremely upset.

Dunny: a toilet. Usually an outside one.

E

Earbashing: when someone endlessly nags you.

F

Fair suck of the sav!: an exclamation of wonder or disbelief ('sav' is short for saveloy, a seasoned sausage, so the person is literally asking for a fair bite of the sausage).

Five-finger discount: to steal something.

Flat chat: to go as fast as possible.

Flat out like a lizard drinking: to be extremely busy.

Flog: to steal something.

Flynn (in like): Named after Errol Flynn, an Australian actor who was a hit with the ladies, this means to 'have an in' with the opposite sex.

Frog in a sock, as cross as a: someone who is extremely angry.

Fruit loop: a fool or crazy person.

G

Galah: an idiot or silly person. Named after the bird of the same name because of its antics and the noise it makes.

Gander: to have a look.

Gasbag: to have a conversation with someone or someone who talks a lot.

Get the shits, give someone the shits: to become annoyed or to annoy someone.

Get up somebody: Don't take this literally! It means to yell at or rebuke someone.

Give it a burl: to try something or give it a go.

Gobful, to give someone a: to verbally abuse someone.

Go crook: to get upset with someone or something.

Good onya: good for you, well done.

Good as gold: something outstanding or something that will be accomplished soon.

Good sport: an agreeable person.

Good sort: an attractive person.

Go walkabout: to go wandering.

Grog: alcohol.

Grouse (mostly used in Victoria): something terrific.

Grumble bum: someone who complains a lot.

H

Happy as Larry: to be particularly pleased with something.

Heaps: to like something a lot.

Hooley Dooley!: Wow! An exclamation of surprise.

Hooroo: see you later.

Hooter: someone's nose or the siren that sounds at the end of a football match.

Humdinger: something that is exceptionally good.

I

Icy pole, ice block: a popsicle or iced lollypop.

Iffy: Something of doubtful origin.

J

Jackaroo: a male 'cowboy' or farm hand.

Jillaroo: a female 'cowgirl' or farm hand.

Joey: baby kangaroo.

K

Keen as mustard: very excited (named after a mustard brand).

Knackered: exhausted.

Knock: to criticise.

Knock back: to refuse something. For example, 'I asked her out but she knocked me back.'

Knocker/ Knockers: somebody who criticises/women's breasts.

L

Larrikin: a person who plays around or makes practical jokes.

Lend of, to have a: to take advantage of someone or to joke.

Lippy: lipstick.

Lollies: sweets, candy.

Longneck: 750ml bottle of beer.

M

Maccas (pron. "mackers"): McDonald's restaurants.

Mate's rates: a cheaper price for a friend.

Milk bar: a corner shop that sells takeaway food (and milk of course!).

Mongrel: someone who has done something wrong.

Moo Juice: milk.

Motza: a hell of a lot.

Mozzie: mosquito.

N

No dramas: same as 'no worries'.

No worries!: It's not a problem.

O

O.S.: overseas.

Ocker: a really 'Australian' person.

Oldies: your parents.

Op shop: an opportunity or thrift shop.

P

Pash: a passionate kiss.

Perve: to check out the opposite sex.

Pearler: something absolutely fantastic.

Piece of piss: something very easy.

Pig's arse: to strongly not agree with something.

Piss/ Pissed: alcohol/ a drunk person. Another one not to be taken literally, especially when someone says, 'he's been drinking piss all day.'

Plate, bring a: instruction on party or BBQ invitation to bring your own food. It doesn't mean they're short of crockery!

Plonk: cheap wine.

Pokies: poker machines, fruit machines – gambling slot machines.

Pom/ Pommy: an Englishman.

Pozzy: position.

Prezzy: a present or gift.

Q

Quid, to make a: to make a living.

R

Reckon!, D'ya reckon?: to think a certain way, to question what someone thinks.

Reffo: a refugee.

Rellie or Relo: one's family relative.

Ridgy-didge: an original or genuine item. Someone who is telling the truth.

Right, she'll be: everything will be okay.

Right, that'd be: something unavoidable or ironic.

Rip snorter: something fantastic.

Ripper: something fantastic.

Rock up: to turn up or arrive. For example, 'we rocked up at their place around 8.'

Ropeable: very angry.

Rort: to cheat or defraud something. In Australia, this term is usually reserved for politicians.

Run Around Like a Headless Chook: to be crazy.

S

Sanga: a sandwich.

Seppo: an American, rhyming slang Yank – Septic Tank, then shortened in the Aussie way to Seppo.

Servo: petrol station.

She'll be right: everything will be okay.

Sheepshagger: a New Zealander.

Sheila: a woman.

Shonky: a product of poor quality.

Shoot through: to leave somewhere.

Skull: to drink an alcoholic beverage in a single go.

Slab: a carton of 24 bottles or cans of beer.

Smoko: a smoke or coffee break.

Snaky: to be upset or irritable.

Sook: a person who whinges or is soft.

Spewin': someone who is very angry.

Spit the dummy: to get very upset.

Spunk: a good looking person (of either sex).

Squiz, to take a: to have a look.

Starkers: naked.

Stickybeak: a nosy person.

Stoked: very pleased. Often used by surfers.

Strewth!: an exclamation of disbelief.

Strides: someone's pants or trousers.

Stubby: a 375ml beer bottle.

Stubby holder: an insulated holder to keep your stubby cold and your hands warm.

Stuffed: to be extremely tired.

Suss: has two meanings. One, to check something out. Two, something suspicious.

T

Taking the piss: another one not to be taken literally. It means to make fun of.

Tea: supper.

Thunderbox: a toilet.

Tinny: both a can of beer and a small boat.

Too right!: you couldn't be more correct!

Troppo: To go crazy, as in gone crazy due to the tropical heat.

True blue: to be patriotic or very accurate or honest.

Turn it up!: to express one's disbelief.

Turps, hit the: to get drunk.

U

Ugg boots: Australian sheepskin boots worn by surfers since at least the 1960s to keep warm while out of the water. Also worn by airmen during the First and Second World Wars because of the need to maintain warmth in non-pressurized planes at high altitudes.

Umpteen: an undefined, yet generally numerous, amount.

Up oneself: to think really highly of one's self.

Ute: a utility vehicle or what Americans would call a pickup truck.

V

Veggies: vegetables.

Veg out: relax in front of the TV, to sit still like a vegetable.

W

Waggin' school: to truant.

Waffle: no, not something you eat. It means to talk on about nothing important.

Walkabout: a walk in the Outback by Aborigines that lasts for an indefinite amount of time

Whacker, whacka: an idiot or crazy person.

Willy Nilly: to act in a reckless manner.

Wingnut: an idiot.

Whinge: to complain.

Wobbly, to chuck a: to get upset about something.

X

XXXX: pronounced Four X, a brand of Queensland beer.

Y

Yakka: to work hard.

Yewy: to turn your car one hundred and eighty degrees.

Yonks: a long period of time, for example, 'I haven't seen him in yonks'.

Yobbo: an uncouth person.

Youse: plural of you.

Z

Zeees: to catch some Zees, to sleep.

Zonk/ Zonked: to be tired or to fall asleep.

Local Knowledge: A Handy Translator

Item	Other Country's Version	Australian Equivalent
Insulated box for keeping food cold	NZ – Chilly Bin US – Cooler	Esky
Convenience Store	NZ – Dairy	Milk bar
Bed quilt	NZ/ UK – Duvet	Doona
Flip- Flops	NZ – Jandals	Thongs
G-String	Thongs	G-Banger
Sweater	NZ – Jersey	Jumper
Swimwear	UK – Trunks US – Trunks NZ – Togs	Swimmers or bathers
Sweat pants	Sweat pants	Trakkies
Peppers	Peppers	Capsicum
Rear compartment of a car	US – Trunk	Boot
Tomato Sauce	US – Ketchup	Tomato Sauce
Plastic Footwear	UK – Flip flops NZ – Jandals	Thongs

What Do We Call Each Other: Differences between the States

The colonial history of Australia, having six separate colonies, has led to many intense rivalries between the states. For example, Canberra, the nation's capital, is where it is (in the middle of nowhere) because Australia's two biggest cities, Sydney and Melbourne, couldn't agree between themselves as to who should be the capital. The solution: build a new city in between.

And the rivalry between Sydney and Melbourne, to this day, is as strong as ever.

Now each person from the separate states has a particular name for people from other states and, in keeping with our call someone a bad name because we love them attitude, our names for people from other states might sound like we hate them, we really don't!

State	Nickname	Origin
New South Wales (The First/ Premier State)	Cockroaches	Presumably, because New South Wales has a plentiful supply of cockroaches.
Queensland (The Sunshine State)	Cane Toads/ Banana Benders	Due to the plague proportions of introduced cane toads and the large number of banana plantations in the Sunshine State.
South Australia (The Festival/ Wine State)	Crow eaters	Due to their state symbol, the crow, appearing on their emblem as if it is on a dinner plate.
Western Australia (The Wildflower/ Golden State)	Sandgropers	With the largest coastline of any state – they have a hell of a lot of sand.
Victoria (The Garden State)	Mexicans	Because they are down south.
Tasmania (The Apple/ Holiday Isle)	Taswegians/ Apple-eaters	After their name, the Apple Isle, due to large numbers of apple orchards on the islands.
Northern Territory (The Top End/ NT)	Territorians/ Croc bait	Because they have hundreds of thousands of huge saltwater and freshwater crocodiles and you can't go in the water in the NT without something killing you!
Australian Capital Territory (The Nation's Capital)	Actarians/ Yogi	Because it is where our Federal politicians are, it could possibly be more dangerous than anywhere else in Australia!

How to Be Mistaken for an Aussie

1. *Talk yourself down* – In Australia we have a phrase called, 'Tall Poppy Syndrome'. What this means is a flower, or Poppy, growing higher than the others, needs to be cut down. Australians don't like when people big note themselves.

2. *Sport is everything* – Australians love to admire those who achieve in sport or anything physical really. So, praise those that do this and, most importantly, make sure you know the difference between the football codes.

3. *Look after your mates* – The embodiment of mateship is no more highlighted than with some of our Victoria Cross Winners. The two most recent of these are Ben Roberts-Smith and Mark Donaldson. Roberts-Smith who, as a sniper, was under severe fire from the Taliban. Roberts-Smith drew enemy fire by putting himself out in the open so his mates would have a chance to survive. Mark Donaldson did the same, protecting his injured mates and to rescue an interpreter. So keep an eye on your mates, keep them out of trouble and if needed, help them out when they need it most.

4. *Be at one with the land* – Aboriginal people have a strong and deep connection with the land. But all Aussies, whether they realise it or not, do too. To be an Aussie you have to show that you have an affinity and respect for 'the bush' and the Outback, and know how to look after yourself.

5. *Drink a cup of concrete* – Another Aussie saying that it not as literal as it may seem. When an Aussie tells you to, 'drink a cup of concrete,' they are actually telling you to, 'harden up.' Basically, this just means accept the way things are without bitching or whinging. So, to be an Aussie, drink up!

6. *Be prepared to make fun of yourself* – Aussies don't take life too seriously, and, we often make jokes at our own expense. If you want to be an Aussie be prepared to talk yourself down. However, don't overdo it because Aussies don't really like this either.

7. *DIY* – Australians are all about Do It Yourself. Even if you have no idea what you are doing, Australians will have a crack at anything. The country is littered with people's DIY projects, some good, some bad, but if you want to be like us just pretend you're an expert.

8. *Understatement is better* – Aussies do respect anyone that achieves big things in life but it is important not to talk yourself up when you do achieve. There's nothing Aussies hate more than someone who is continually big noting themselves. If you receive a compliment, your best bet is to just politely say, 'thank you,' and leave it at that.

9. *Treat everyone as an equal* – Aussies are not concerned about where you went to school, how rich you are or what your job is. We might ask you about work, or something else, but we are really more worried about whether you're a good bloke or sheila. To fit in as an Aussie, treat everyone on the same level.

10. *Bring beer to a barbie* – If you truly want to make yourself loved by an Aussie and to fit right in as one, when you're invited to a barbie turn up with beer (or any other form of alcohol will do). The fit in even further, leave any alcohol that you haven't drunk at your guests' house as a sign that you have enjoyed their barbie.

How to Eat Like an Aussie

Traditional Australian cuisine, fifty years ago, consisted of meat and two veg (which also forms an unfortunate slang term for the male private parts). This was due, in part, to our Britishness, the two World Wars and the Depression made a variety of ingredients sparse and unavailable.

With the influx of migrants over the last century or so, we have readily taken to everything from pizza and lasagne, to traditional Chinese food and Thai food. In fact, Spaghetti Bolognese has become a quintessential Australian favourite (of course, in the Australian way, we have reduced this to Spag Bol).

Australia doesn't have too many foods that we can claim as our own but there are a few that we have made, or made our own...

The Vegemite Sandwich

You either love Vegemite or you hate it. It is a strange concoction of black yeast and Vitamin B that we spread on our toast and put on sandwiches for our school lunches. Other versions include Marmite or Promite but, if you ask any Aussie, nothing compares.

The Meat Pie

Another Aussie favourite, the meat pie is usually eaten in one hand with tomato sauce. A pie is not a pie unless the tomato sauce is dripping down your hand and the mince and gravy from the pie is dribbling across your fingers. Oh, and of course, the pie must be hot enough that it burns your mouth.

Sausage Roll

Sausage meat wrapped in pastry, a sausage roll has to be eaten with tomato sauce. It is a handy lunch meal because it can be eaten with one hand.

A Hamburger with the Lot

The humble hamburger takes on a life of its own in Australia. The traditional cheeseburger, if it is to be truly Aussie, needs to have lettuce, tomato, the usual, but it also must have beetroot (yes, beetroot) pineapple, bacon and a fried egg. Again, the burger is not eaten in the correct fashion unless the yoke of the egg is dripping down your fingers.

Chicko/ Spring Roll

A spring roll is similar to a Chinese spring roll wrapped in batter. The Chicko Roll was inspired by the spring roll, it is a mixture of vegetables and beef. It was made with a deliberately thick outer layer so it could be eaten in the hand at the football without it completely falling apart. Strangely, even though it bears the name Chicko Roll it has no chicken!

Chicken Parmi

A chicken schnitzel covered in toasted cheese, sometimes with ham or bacon, or anything else you can think to put on top of it.

Prawns

First of all, let's set one thing straight, in Australia we do not, repeat, do not, call prawns 'shrimps'! What started as a campaign to promote Australia to the United States through one of our comedic icons, Paul Hogan, has now led to the most cringe worthy phrases an Aussie can hear.

Prawns can be enjoyed at any time of the year but they are most eaten as part of Christmas lunch. Prawns, not shrimps. Repeat. Prawns, not shrimps.

Prawn Cocktail

The Prawn Cocktail is a common entrée for Aussies or a healthy, tasty summer lunch. The sauce is really what makes this.

Method

1 iceberg lettuce, washed and shredded.
600 grams (or whatever amount you decide) of cooked, peeled prawns.

Cocktail Sauce

If you wanted to cheat you can just buy seafood sauce from the supermarket but if you want to try the 'real' Australian recipe make the sauce in the following manner:

60 ml (¼ cup) of Tomato Sauce.
60 ml (¼ cup) of thin cream.
1 tablespoon of fresh lemon juice.
1 teaspoon Worcestershire sauce.
Dash of Tabasco sauce.
Freshly ground salt and pepper.

Method

1. Combine the tomato sauce, cream, lemon juice, Worcestershire sauce and Tabasco in a small bowl. Taste and season with salt and pepper.
2. Place the lettuce on a serving plate or in a glass. Top with the prawns and drizzle with the cocktail sauce.

Fish and Chips/Calamari

There is nothing better than going down to a great Aussie beach and grabbing yourself a serving of fish and chips. Most Australia fish is shark wrapped in batter so, if fish is not your go, crumbed calamari makes an equally tasty accompaniment.

Balmain Bugs/Moreton Bay Bugs

This small lobster without claws is bloody tasty but mostly eaten as part of a quality Aussie Christmas dinner.

Sausage (Snags)

In keeping with the laziness of our language a sausage 'sanga' is, in fact, a sausage sandwich. A staple of the Australian diet and a golden fundraiser for charities and schools across the country, a sausage or two between a slice of bread or two is the backbone of any decent Aussie BBQ. You do have a choice between BBQ or tomato sauce and fried onions are optional but, again, the sandwich must be so full that the sauce covers your fingers and you struggle to keep the contents of the sandwich within the confines of the bread.

Damper

Damper is a form of Australian bush bread. Many Outback workers lived off this stuff back in the day but now most Aussies only make it on camping trips.

Recipe for Damper on an Open-fire

450 grams (3 cups) of self-raising flour.
A pinch of salt.
80 grams of butter, chilled, cubed.
185 ml (¾ cup) of milk (water will suffice if you have no milk).

Method

1. Mix the flour, salt and sugar together into a bowl.
2. Rub the butter into the flour with your fingertips until it looks like fine breadcrumbs.

3. Add milk (or water) slowly and mix together to form a soft dough.
4. Knead lightly on a floured board until smooth. Shape into a round loaf, brush with milk and cut a cross in the top surface of the dough.
5. Grease a camp oven (if you have one, aluminium foil will also suffice) and dust with flour. Add bread dough and cover (if only aluminium foil is available wrap the bread dough entirely. It is important not to leave any areas exposed, as this will blacken that part of the bread).
6. Place in the campfire, cover with hot ashes and coals and bake for about 30 minutes.

Weet-Bix
Developed in the 1930s, these simple wheat biscuits have been a staple diet for Australians ever since. The question is usually 'how many can you eat?' Australians are often called Weet-Bix kids. Serve with some bananas or strawberries.

Aussie Treats

A Gaytime
Australians love a Gaytime! Contrary to what this might conjure up in modern day parlance, a Gaytime is not what it sounds like. It is in fact a toffee and vanilla ice cream dipped in chocolate and wrapped in honeycomb biscuits.

Pavlova
A meringue based desert that is covered in as many fruits as you can manage to fit on it but mostly strawberries and kiwi fruit. It has a crispy crust and a marshmallow inside. Now, there has been a constant argument between the Aussies and the Kiwis about who invented the Pavlova but one thing that is certain it was named after the Russian ballerina, Anna Pavlova, who was touring Australia and New Zealand in the 1920s when the 'pav' was invented.

Chocolate Crackles

A favourite amongst Aussie kids, particularly at birthday parties, every adult also sneaks a Chocolate Crackle too. They are a simple mix of chocolate and rice bubbles. Easy to make and delicious to eat!

Ingredients

4 cups of rice bubbles.
1 cup icing sugar.
1 cup desiccated coconut.
3 tablespoons of cocoa.
250g copha, chopped.

Method

In a large bowl, mix the rice bubbles, icing sugar, cocoa and coconut.

Slowly melt the copha in a saucepan over a low heat then allow the mixture to slightly cool.

Take melted copha and add it to the rice bubble mix.

Keep stirring until it is well and truly combined.

Take spoonfuls of the final mix, place them in paper patty cases and refrigerate until firm.

Twisties

Twisties are probably representative of the Australian sense of humour. Twisties are made from corn, rice, wheat and water. In 1950, a businessman from Melbourne made the first attempts at making a corn-based snack. He was unsuccessful and agreed to sell the machine he had been using and the brand to Monty Lea, of the Darrell Lea Company, who after several experiments with the machine successfully made Twisties. The high temperature heating process is what gives Twisties their distinctive shape.

Fairy Bread

A perennial favourite at kid's parties, Fairy Bread is nothing more than buttered bread with sprinkled hundreds and thousands on top. Kids adore the stuff, but parents and other adults will always relive their childhood by grabbing a few sneaky slices.

Lamingtons
A quintessential Aussie desert, particularly favoured by older ladies, the lamington is a square sponge cake. Wrapped in chocolate and coconut, lamingtons make the perfect morning tea.

Caramel Slice
A classic Australia treat, a caramel slice is a biscuit and coconut base with a caramel centre and a layer of dark chocolate on top. Warning: be careful when trying caramel slice for the first time because you will be tempted to have more!

Aussie Bikkies (Biscuits)
We all know that nothing beats Mum's home cooking and, short of finding a generic recipe, my mum makes the best ANZAC biscuits (biscuits or cookies that are made from rolled oats) I have ever eaten so, with her permission, here is her recipe but guard it closely!

ANZAC Biscuits
By Christine Foster

Ingredients

1 cup rolled oats.
¾ cup of coconut.
1 cup of self-raising flour.
1 ½ teaspoons of bicarbonate of soda.
2 tablespoons of boiling water.
1 cup of sugar.
½ cup (125g) of butter.
1 tablespoon of Golden Syrup.

Method

Mix oats, flour, sugar and coconut together. In a small saucepan melt syrup and butter together. Mix bicarbonate of soda with boiling water, then add the melted butter and syrup. Add to the dry ingredients. Place one tablespoon of the mixture on greased baking trays.

Bake in moderate oven (180°C) for 15-20 minutes or till browned. Biscuits will harden as they cool.

Iced Vo Vo
An Aussie classic, the Vo Vo has a biscuit base with lines of pink frosting on the outside, a line of raspberry jam in the middle and coconut sprinkled on top.

Sao
Another classic Aussie treat! It is actually nothing more than a dry biscuit but is fantastic with tomato, cheese and avocado. The name Sao apparently comes from the fact that the biscuits used to be handed out to people by Salvation Army Officers (SAO).

Australia's Best Chokkies (Chocolates)
Cherry Ripe
Arguably, Australia's favourite chocolate bar, the Cherry Ripe is our oldest chocolate bar and also the highest selling chocolate bar. A rich tasting treat that is desiccated cherry and coconut wrapped in dark chocolate.

Wagon Wheel
Travellers to Australia often become confused as to why an Australian treat would have the name of a Wild West stagecoach. The Wagon Wheel is basically a marshmallow sandwich. The chocolate has two biscuits with a marshmallow centre, wrapped in chocolate. The name comes from the shape of the biscuits themselves but also after the last name of the inventor, Garry Weston.

Fantales

A semi-hard caramel centre wrapped in chocolate. Fantales were highly popular in the past, eaten whilst at the Saturday movie matinees. The association with Fantales and the cinema has continued to this day and every individual Fantales wrapper has trivia about movies and movies stars.

Jaffas

Jaffas, invented in 1931, are another perennial movie favourite and kids always have fun rolling the little red balls down the cinema (aisle) or on the school bus. Jaffas have a crispy red shell and orange-flavoured chocolate insides. The name, thus, coming from the Jaffa orange.

Caramello Koala

Caramello Koalas have been delighting Aussie kids since 1966. Caramello Koala, or 'George', is a koala shaped chocolate with a caramel centre. Caramello Koalas are a popular fundraiser and over 40 million are sold each year, making it Australia's second most popular children's chokkie.

Freddo Frog

The most popular children's chokkie. Created in 1930 by Harry Melbourne for MacRoberston chocolates, as unthinkable as it would be to Aussies today, Freddo actually started life out as a mouse. Thankfully, Harry knew a frog would sell!

Tim Tams

Tim Tams are an Australian icon and any Australian living overseas will always miss these. Tim Tams are also the biscuit that overseas travellers immediately adore! Made by the iconic Australia biscuit brand, Arnott's, the Tim Tam is made of two chocolate malted biscuits with a light chocolate cream filling and the whole thing is coated in chocolate.

Tim Tams were created when Ian Norris, director of technology at Arnott's, went to Britain and encountered the Penguin biscuit. On trying the Penguin, he decided he was going to come back to Australia and invent a 'better one.' (Maybe the fact we one-upped the Poms is another reason we love these biscuits!).

Tim Tams hit the shops in 1964. Most Aussies probably won't know this but Tim Tams were named so after Ross Arnott went to the 1958 Kentucky Derby and decided the winner, Tim Tam, was a top name for a bikkie!

One of the best ways to enjoy a Tim Tam is to break the end off, stick it in your coffee, and suck! There are many attempts to substitute the Tim Tam but nothing else compares.

Violet Crumble

A Violet Crumble has a crumbly, honeycomb centre wrapped in chocolate. It is similar (but, from an Australian perspective, way better than a Crunchie). The slogan for the chocolate bar has become an Australian classic, 'it's the way it shatters that matters!' referring to the honeycomb centre.

A jam maker, Abel Hoadley, who expanded into chocolate treats, invented the bar. His wife's favourite colour was purple and her favourite flower, the violet, so, as a good Aussie hubby does, he packages his treats in the missus' favourite colour. One of the treats was honeycomb and, this being the most popular, he made this into an individual bar.

The Violet Crumble still has purple packaging to this day.

Bush Tucker

The Witchetty Grub

A strange looking caterpillar larva, Aboriginal Australians have been enjoying this little delicacy for thousands of years. Witchetty grubs taste good both cooked and raw and have a nut-like flavour.

Yabby

Yabbies are freshwater crayfish. There are little blue ones that look like mini-lobsters and the big red ones are very similar to their saltwater cousins. They are bloody tasty, especially with a beer or a glass of wine.

Kangaroo

Yes, we eat kangaroo! We eat kangaroo steaks and kangaroo snags! We may just be the only country in the world that eats their national symbol (we even eat emu too!).

Crocodile

Crocodile meat tastes very much like chicken (it can also have a slight fishy smell) and can be prepared like chicken.Research has shown crocodile meat is a healthier choice than our regular meats and is also high in potassium and magnesium.

How to Cook Like an Aussie

Simple.

Take whatever you have and throw it on the barbie.

Drink a few stubbies or a couple of glasses of chardy. Make a salad. Burn the shit out of everything you put on the barbie and you're good.

If someone asks you to 'bring a plate' to a barbie, don't take it literally! It means bring a plate of food; usually a salad or desert will suffice.

However, if you want to step it up a notch.

Anything roasted, particularly lamb, with some nice roast veggies like pumpkin or potato are also Aussie favourites.

How to Dress Like an Aussie

Aussie fashion is unique, based around our landscape and climate, it is fun, yet practical, desirable yet durable. Collette Dinnigan, Alex Perry, Carla Zampatti, these are the names that have showcased our fashions to the world. Let's get it straight. Summer in Australia is incredibly hot and winters can be incredibly cold. Hence, in the winter we wear a lot of clothes but, in the summer, we generally wear as little as possible.

Winter

Winter fashions can range from the chic and fashionable to the downright despicable, either way their purpose is to keep us warm. Foreign visitors might assume that Australia is always hot but winter in Australia can get cold, damn cold. People wear woollen jackets and long coats as well as jumpers and jackets.

Ugg Boots

Ugg boots are sheepskin boots with fleece on the inside; they have been around, in some form, since the 1920s. There is controversy over who were the first designers of the boot. Blue Mountains Ugg boots claim they have been making them since 1933. Whereas Frank Mortel of Mortel's Sheepskin Factory claims he made them in the late 1950s and named the boots because his wife called them 'ugly'. Other variations in this are that the boots came from 'fug' boots, which pilots wore to keep their feet warm in the First World War.

Ugg boots found worldwide fame when American surfers came to Australia and saw our surfers wearing the boots to keep their feet warm and adopted the practice.

Ugg boots, as a fashion statement, have gone through several stages. They started as a sign of rebellion, moved to being associated with lower class people, like bogans and westies, and then back to being fashionable among the broader population.

Many other companies and countries have tried to imitate the Ugg Boot but nothing compares to the Australia original.

Summer
Men

Boardies and thongs (flip-flops) are the order of the day and, generally, a T-shirt. Australian summer wear, naturally, revolves around beachwear and some of our famous brands have become worldwide names such as Rip Curl, Billabong and Quicksilver. At night, these brands have more formal shirts and usually this with a pair of jeans will suffice.

Women

Aussie girls generally wear shorts and a short or singlet top. Many girls wear dresses with sandals.

What to Wear and How to Take Care?

Australian clothing and fashion is strongly determined by the people we are and the country we live in. As a result, Australian clothing is both stylish yet practical but we're also happy to take designs from other countries when it suits us.

The two things that make us Aussies are the bush and the beach and, therefore, our main forms of dress and clothing reflect this.

Essential Beach Wear and Items

Cossies (Swim wear)

Women – bikini or a one-piece swimsuit. Ladies usually take large hats to the beach to protect them from the fierce Aussie sun.

Men – Boardies come in a variety of colours and double not only as shorts but also as swim wear.

Budgie Smugglers (Speedos) – VERY optional!

Rashie (Rash vest) – Surfers and body-boarders often wear these to protect themselves from rubbing against their boards. Other people also wear these to protect themselves from the sun.

Thongs or sandals – these are a must! There is nothing worse when the temperature is over 40 degrees Celsius (104 degrees Fahrenheit) and trying to walk on hot roads or even hotter sand.

50+ SPF Sunscreen – it might seem strange to include sunscreen as something to wear but it is a must to 'wear' sunscreen in the Australian summer. Australia has the highest rate of melanoma (skin cancer) in the world and the average person will begin to burn after only ten minutes in the Aussie sun.

The Bush

Akubra Hat – The iconic wide-brimmed hat is made from rabbit fur (so, in true Aussie style, we even use a pest to our advantage!). The word 'Akubra' is believed to be an Aboriginal word for headwear and it has been an icon of the Australian bush for nearly 130 years. The hat was heavily featured in the opening ceremony of the 2000 Sydney Olympics. The hat is actually presented to visiting dignitaries as a gift. The Akubra is used to shield from the sun, brush away flies, fan fires and the list goes on.

Driza-Bone – The Driza-Bone is a long, full-length, waterproof riding coat. A rearrangement of the phrase 'Dry-as-a-bone', the word is a trademark of an Aussie company that has been making the iconic long coat since 1898.

Flannelette Shirt – The Flannelette shirt, or 'Flanno', is made from wool, cotton or synthetic fibre. Originally made from Scottish flannel, the Flanno is used to describe any shirt of plaid or tartan patterns. Farmers and stockmen often wear them in the country. In the city, it is considered to be more of a 'bogan', or lower class, shirt.

Local Knowledge: How to Stay Safe at the Beach

Popular Australian beaches will have two red and yellow chequered flags on them, which indicate to the public the safest area to swim. The lifeguards put the flags out, these guys are the best qualified to know where to swim, so it's best to heed their advice. However, if you do get in serious trouble raise your hand and yell loudly until you attract the attention of the lifeguards and they will rush out to rescue you.

One of the most dangerous things at the beach (way more dangerous than sharks or stingers) is riptides. 'Rips', as Aussies call them, are strong currents that can quickly pull you out to sea. Rips are characterised by:

- Choppy channels of water.
- Lines of seaweed or debris.
- Disrupted waves.

A couple of simple rules to remember:

- Keep yourself as calm as you can. It is important not to struggle because you will tire yourself out.

- Do not, under ANY circumstances, try to swim against the rip. Rips are very strong and you can still get pulled out and you will tire yourself out. Your best bet is to swim sideways, parallel to the beach, until you are out of the rip and you can make your way back to shore. Ensure you swim on an angle because rips can change their position very quickly.
- If you are unable to do this, tread water or float. Rips weaken as they go out to sea. Once you are out of the rip swim sideways again and then back into the shore.

How to Drink Like an Aussie

Australians have a reputation around the world for being prolific drinkers, mostly of beer, but Australian drinking culture is often complex and highly ritualised. One Australian tradition the foreign traveller needs to know is the 'shout'.

The shout is not someone calling out as loud as they can but a drinking ritual whereby one person will buy a 'round' of drinks. Now, it gets a little hazy from here. You are expected to 'shout back', to buy someone a drink or a round of drinks if they have brought you one, but sometimes, if you finish drinking before a round is complete it is acceptable to not shout back but you are expected to remember that someone has shouted you a drink and to buy them one back at the next available moment.

The History of Drinking

Australia's drinking laws were pretty relaxed in the beginning but, by 1916, the laws tightened up. Pubs were forced to close at 6pm which led to such things as the, 'Six o'clock Swill'. Workers generally finished as five o'clock and, after work, they had around an hour to drink. They would binge drink and it led to many social problems. Sundays and long hours, particularly with the Temperance movement, led to a no-go for drinking on the Sabbath and for extended hours.

Women, however, were not allowed to drink in public bars. In a typical Australian act of feminism, Merle Thomas and Rosalie Bogner chained themselves to the Regatta Hotel. While the publican faced heavy fines if he served them, many sympathetic male drinkers brought the girls a drink. This simple act is seen as one of the major feminist protests in Australian history.

Beer in Australia

Firstly, beer in Australia is much more of a minefield than an overseas visitor would expect. Let's get something straight. The most famous Australian beer is Foster's but no-one, in Australia drinks it! In fact, you would be hard pressed to find an Australian that actually drinks Foster's. Perhaps, again due to our colonial heritage, each Australian state has its own brand of beer and own name for it. If you are in one state and you ask for a type or size of beer from another state, the bartender may have absolutely no idea what you are talking about.

A Visitor's Guide to Aussie Beers

State of Australia	Beer of Choice/ Brand Name	Name of a Glass of Beer
New South Wales	Tooheys New/ Reschs	Schooner (425ml)/ Middy (325ml)
Queensland	XXXX	Pot (285ml)
Victoria	Victoria Bitter	Pot (285ml)
South Australia	West End/ Coopers	Pot/ Schooner/ Pint
Western Australia	Swan Lager	Pot (The size of a Pint!)
Tasmania	Cascade/ Boag's	7/10/12 ounce
Northern Territory	Darwin Stubbie	2 litre beer!!

Local Knowledge: You Know it is Hot in Australia when...

1. Your thongs (the ones you wear on your feet) melt on the road.
2. Your car seat belt leaves burn marks or brands on your skin.
3. You can't hold the steering wheel or you have to drive with two fingers.
4. You can fry an egg on the engine of your car.

5. Hot water comes out of the hose or out of both taps.
6. When you get out of the shower and you need another one 5 minutes later.
7. You dance like a crazy person when walking across any hard surface in bare feet.
8. When even the wildlife need a drink!
9. You need to put a jumper on when the temperature drops below 25 degrees.
10. You can't sleep because the air-con makes you sick and you're too sunburnt to move.

Chapter Six:

A National Obsession:
Sport in Australia

Australians love their sports! Football in the winter and cricket in the summer are the main two sports but, as Aussies, we love swimming, tennis, golf, pretty much everything.

However, a person visiting from another country might need some tips to understand both sports.

The Summer Passion: Cricket

For the uninitiated, cricket can seem *incredibly* confusing. An Aussie discussing the cricket might start talking to you about square legs, silly points, slashing outside off, running it down to third man, bowling a Chinaman or a Googly, delivering a jaffa or throwing down a pie.

As our national sport, if you want to get into a conversation with an Aussie about the cricket there are a few things you need to know... Cricket developed in the 19th century and has since spread to many countries around the world (mostly, ex-British colonies such as Australia, New Zealand, South Africa and India).

Cricket is somewhat similar to baseball. You have two batters who are trying to hit a ball. When they hit the ball they run. A run is scored when a batsman safely completes the 22 yards to the opposite end of the pitch. The other batsman then takes his turn to 'take strike' or to prepare himself to hit the ball. Batsman can score single, double or triple runs in this fashion. If a batsman hits the ball and it bounces one or more times and reaches the boundary (the edge of the field) the batsman is awarded four runs. If a batsman hits the ball over the fence without it bouncing, he is awarded six runs. A batsman will try to complete as many runs as they can safely, 50 runs is a good milestone, with a century (or 100 runs) the ultimate milestone for any batsman.

At each end of the pitch are wickets or stumps, three wooden poles. On top of these are the bails (two small pieces of wood). The batsman's aim is to protect these stumps whilst still scoring runs.

Each team has eleven batsman, but the batting team must have two batsman on the pitch, so an innings ends after ten batsman are out or dismissed.

How to get dismissed in cricket

At the opposite end of a cricket pitch you have a bowler (pitcher) whose job is to launch (bowl) the ball and attempt to dismiss the batsman. There are eleven ways a fielding team can do this, they are as follows:

Bowled – when a bowler hits the stumps, and the bails are removed when the ball hits them.

Caught – when a batsman hits a ball to a fielder and that fielder catches the ball on the full.

Leg Before Wicket – in the early days, batsman were using their legs to stop the ball hitting the stumps so the LBW (Leg Before Wicket) rule was introduced. What this means is that if (in the opinion of the umpire) the batsman has been hit on the legs and the ball was likely to go on and hit the stumps, then that batsman is dismissed.

Run Out – when the batsmen are attempting to complete a run, there is a white line to indicate when the run is complete. If a member of the fielding team hits the wickets with the ball and the batsman is short of the crease when the bails are dislodged, then the batsman is dismissed.

Stumped – this is the same as a run out, but it is when the bowler has delivered the ball and the batsman has a) missed it and b) is out of his crease. If the wicketkeeper (the same as a catcher in baseball) has the ball in his hand and dislodges the bails without the batsman returning to his crease, then he is dismissed.

Hit Wicket – when a batsman attempts to hit the ball, if any part of his body or his bat dislodges the bails from the wicket, he is dismissed.

Retired Hurt – cricket is a dangerous game. The leather ball hurts when it hits you and batsman will wear padding on their legs, hands, arms and elbows, along with a helmet, to avoid getting hurt. However, injuries still happen and if a batsman is injured and feels like he cannot continue he can opt to, 'retire hurt.'

Handled the Ball – if a batsman has attempted to hit the ball and it is moving towards the wickets a batsman is permitted to deflect the ball away from the wickets with his bat or any part of his body, except his hands. Should the batsman use his hands he is dismissed.

Obstructing the Field – simply put, if the batsman attempts to interfere with a fielder or the bowler whilst that player in trying to effect a dismissal then the batsman is dismissed.

Hitting the Ball Twice – this means that if the ball has hit the batsman's body or his bat and he attempts to hit it again before a fielder has touched it, then he is dismissed. The only time a batsman is allowed to strike the ball twice is if the batter is defending their wicket from the ball hitting it or if, with the permission of the fielding team, they are returning the ball to the opposition.

Timed Out – whilst this form of dismissal is very rare, it does happen. After one batsman is dismissed, the subsequent batsman has three minutes to be in position to receive the next bowl. If he is not in position, then he is dismissed.

The Name of the Game

There are three forms of cricket.

Test Cricket

The traditional form of cricket, Test cricket is, as it sounds, meant to be a test for a player. Players wear white and use a red ball. A Test match can last up to five days, yes, five days and, after that time, the game still might end in a draw!

The biggest rivalry Australia has in this form of cricket (or any cricket) is with the Old Enemy, England. The Test series between the two nations is known as *The Ashes*.

One-Day Internationals

In the early 80s a great Australian businessman/ entrepreneur, Kerry Packer, devised a form of cricket which was termed 'limited' overs cricket. Instead of unlimited overs the game was reduced to 50 overs per team (innings). Players also began to wear coloured clothing. Packer's innovations caused much controversy amongst the traditionalists but one-day cricket is now a popular form of the game.

Twenty – 20 Cricket

A shorter version of a one-day international, with only 20 overs per team, T20 cricket is fast-paced and exciting. Many people find the longer forms of the game drawn out and boring so T20 is perfect. T20 is also very popular amongst families for the same reason.

Local Knowledge: The Ashes

The Ashes is the biggest sporting competition between Australia and England. If you were to ask most Aussies whether we would want to win the Ashes or a dozen Olympic Gold Medals, they would probably say to beat the Poms in the Ashes (although if we won a dozen gold medals and the Poms won less than us that would also be good!).

The Ashes takes place, approximately, every two years and it alternates between being played in England and Australia. The contest has delivered some of the greatest moments and achievements in the sport of cricket.

Australia holds all the records with the most series wins (32), the most individual runs (Don Bradman – 5028) and most wickets (Shane Warne – 195).

The Tradition

In the early days of England v Australia, the Aussies were, let's say, getting thumped. We were the easy beats, a bit of a laughing stock. However, in 1882, the touring Australian team claimed their first Test win at the Oval, London. The British paper, the *Sporting Times*, expressing the shock and disbelief of their nation, described the win as the death of English cricket and, as such, published a mock obituary. The obituary said that English cricket had died and, 'the body will be cremated and the ashes taken to Australia.'

When the English came down under to reclaim the Ashes, they did so, winning two out of the three Tests. In response, some Australian women presented a small urn, which reputedly have the remains of burnt bails inside signifying the 'death' of Australian cricket.

The Ashes themselves and the urn are kept at the home of cricket, Lord's in London, but the winning teams hold a replica aloft to signify their victory.

The Winter Passions: Footy (Football)

Using the term 'football', in most countries, would immediately conjure up the traditional type of football – soccer. However, Australia has four codes of football: soccer, rugby league, rugby union and Australian Rules Football.

Geography plays a major part in the type of football you support or play.

Soccer – played across the country.

Rugby Union and Rugby League – both played across the country but they are most popular in New South Wales and Queensland.

Australian Rules – the main form of football in Victoria, Tasmania, Western Australia, South Australia and the Northern Territory but is also popular in New South Wales and Queensland, making it the true national code.

Soccer

Soccer is the mostly widely played form of football in the country but, until recently, soccer has not had a high profile in Australia. Until 2002, Australia had not qualified for the World Cup since 1974, but with qualification and some success (we reached the Round of 16, our best result in the World Cup) and with the development of the national league (the A-League) soccer has now become popular as a spectator sport.

Rugby Union

Rugby traces its origins as far back as the 12th century and, due to the violent nature of the early forms (even resulting in deaths) it was banned in England between the 14th and 17th centuries. The official rules, however, were written down in 1845. The Rugby Football Union was formed in 1871.

There is debate about whether, in the earlier forms, players carried the ball or not but the tradition that has stuck makes for a good yarn nevertheless. The story goes that a schoolboy, William Webb Ellis was in the town of Rugby and...

'Who with fine disregard for the rules of football as played in his time first took the ball in his arms and ran with it, thus originating the distinctive feature of the rugby game.'

The town in which this occurred gives its name to the code and Webb Ellis' actions have earned him the right to have the Rugby Union World cup Trophy named after him.

Rugby union is a complex sport and can be difficult for the uninitiated. A few simple explanations of the rules might help.

Players per team – 15.

Points for a try (placing the ball down over the goal or try line) – 5

Points for a goal – 2

Points for a field goal – 3

Rugby League

Rugby Union was, and has been up until 1995, an amateur sport. The idea for Rugby League first came about in 1895 after some rugby union players decided they were entitled to be paid for their services.

When the Rugby Union authorities declined the players broke away and created their own form of the game. They changed many of the rules to create a more fast-paced and spectator friendly game. Rugby League is, generally, considered to be one of the toughest, full-contact sports in the world. Rugby League began in Australia in 1908.

Players per team – 13

Points for a try – 4

Points for a goal – 2

Points for a field goal – 1

Australian Rules Football

Originally developed as a means of keeping cricketer's fit in the winter time, Australian Rules Football (AFL) is similar to Gaelic Football and can be traced back to 1858 where the first match was played between the Melbourne Grammar School and Scotch College. In 1859, the Melbourne Football Club first penned the official rules of the game. Each Australian Football League (AFL) team is made up of 18 players and is played on an oval shaped field (or a cricket field).

The aim of AFL is to kick the ball through the centre posts. AFL fields have four white posts at each end. If the ball is kicked between the two centre posts a team is awarded 6 points (a goal). If the ball goes to the left or right of the posts on either the right or left sides then a team is awarded 1 point (a behind).

A common scoreboard would look something like this:

Team	Goals	Behinds	Total
Sydney Swans	14	12	106
Collingwood Magpies	11	10	76

Players can kick or handpass (hitting the ball with one fist) the ball to one another or they can run with it. If a player catches the ball on the full he is awarded a mark and he has a chance to kick the ball to another player without interference.

An interesting part of Aussie Rules is that, due to the similarity between Aussie Rules and Gaelic football, the only international match that an AFL player can participate in is Australia vs. Ireland in a modified rules game.

Names of Australian Sporting Teams

Australian sporting teams have names that reflect the animals of our country or something else that is important to us. It can be a minefield but it is vitally important you refer to the right team with the right name. The following is only a list of the main sporting teams in Australia.

Sport	Team	Name
Rugby League	Men	Kangaroos
Rugby League	Women	Jillaroos (named after female 'cowboys')
Basketball	Men	Boomers (a slang term for kangaroos)
Basketball	Women	Opals (a colourful gem only found in Australia, much like our women)

Sport	Team	Name
Hockey	Men	Kookaburras
Hockey	Women	Hockeyroos
Rugby Union	Men	Wallabies
Rugby Union	Women	Wallaroos
Cricket	Men	None
Cricket	Women	Southern Stars
Football	Men	Socceroos
Football	Women	Matildas
Netball	Women	Diamonds

The National Australian Colours

Australia's national colours are green and gold and these two colours create much nationalistic pride and patriotism in Australians.

The general knowledge of the reason for these colours is that the gold represents the national flower, the wattle, and the green our forests and eucalyptus trees. However, the gold also represents our golden beaches and other things like our minerals and one of our main exports/ crops, wheat. The green also represents the rainforest and other greeneries of our landscape.

Whilst green and gold has been the popular colours to represent Australia since the 1800s, it was not until 1984 that they were officially recognised as our national colours. Prior to this a mixture of red, white and blue, or blue and gold were also acceptable.

Great Moments in Australian Sport

Australia has had many great sporting achievements, too many to list here, but there are some that stand out more than others. Aussies love our national heroes and we also love to support the underdog or the battler. This list includes mostly those that have inspired the nation or those that have triumphed over the greatest odds and achieved the unachievable.

The America's Cup

One of the greatest days for Australia in the sporting arena came in September 1983.

The America's Cup yacht race had been won by America (and the New York Yacht Club) for 132 years. *Australia II* (out of the Royal Perth Yacht Club) faced up against the American boat, *Liberty*, at Newport, Rhode Island. Alan Bond paid for the boat and John Bertrand skippered it. However, the key success was the winged-keel design of Ben Lexcen.

Liberty won the first, second and fourth races but *Australia II* came back to win the third, fifth and sixth races. In an amazing seventh race, *Australia II* was victorious.

Back home, just before dawn, all of Australia watched and then celebrated when we won. During the celebrations the then Prime Minister, Bob Hawke, declared, 'any boss who sacks anyone for not turning up today is a bum!'

Cathy Freeman Wins Gold

Cathy Freeman is one of Australia's greatest sprinters and a wonderful ambassador for Indigenous Australians, having won numerous gold medals at both World Championships level and at the Commonwealth Games in the 400m sprint. Freeman won silver at the 1996 Atlanta Olympics so, coming into her home games in Sydney, 2000, she was under tremendous pressure to go one better. Freeman lit the Olympic flame and, from that moment on, the eyes of the nation were upon her. And she didn't let us down, winning gold in the 400m final!

The 1948 Invincibles

The Australian government officially referred to the *Invincibles* as 'one of Australia's most cherished sporting legends.' Widely considered as our greatest ever cricket team, the *Invincibles* get their name from the fact that they went through an *entire* tour of England without losing a match. Captained by Sir Donald Bradman, they played 34 games (31 first-class and 3 non-first class, including 5 Test matches). In the 144 days they were on tour they played for 112 days. They won 25 first-class games and drew 9. Of the 5 Test matches series, they won 4 and drew one.

Cadel Evans

Cadel Evans, nicknamed 'Cuddles', is renowned across Australia as a gritty, determined competitor. Evans has won gold medals and world championships, so we've always known he was good. An Australian had never won the Tour de France, so when Evans finished second in the Tour in both 2007 and 2008 we were proud of him but, as a country, we resigned ourselves to having to wait for an Aussie winner. Then, with true Cadel determination, he won the Tour de France in 2011.

Adam Scott

Australia has an extremely long and proud golfing history but a string of major tournaments has seemed to elude us. Our best player in recent years, Greg Norman, won the British Open but had failed to win any of the American majors. Other Aussies claimed the US Open and the US PGA but the big one, the US Masters, had eluded us. That was until 2013 when Adam Scott broke one of Australia's longest hoodoos. The country watched in the early morning as he faced a play-off and sunk a monster putt to claim the title.

Steven Bradbury's Gold Medal in Skating

Given that Australia is such a hot country and we have a very small Alpine area, winning gold medals at the Winter Olympics was not our particular forte. That was until the Salt Lake City Games of 2002. The story gets better, Bradbury was sitting in fourth place in the 1000m race and, somewhat miraculously, two skaters collided and then took out a third until all the other racers were on the ice. Bradbury glided by and claimed victory.

However, it should be pointed out that Bradbury had claimed bronze in a previous Olympics and had won a gold medal in the World Championships so his good luck did come from hard work.

Great Sporting Controversies

Bodyline (Cricket)

The greatest cricketer of all time, Donald Bradman, averaging 99.94, was spanking the Poms (Mother England) all over the park. So, when the Poms toured Australia for the 1932/33 Ashes series, England captain, Douglas Jardine, decided on a method to get Bradman out or, at least, limit the amount of runs he could score with Leg-theory bowling. What this basically meant was to bowl fast and short to the batsman's leg side (deliberately trying to hit the batsman on the body).

This tactic, whilst legal in the rules of the game at the time, was considered not in the gentlemanly spirit of the game and created much ill will (even at a diplomatic level) between the two nations.

Bodyline bowling led to a change in the laws of cricket and was outlawed. Almost a century later this still causes much ill feeling.

Trevor Chappell's Underarm Ball

In 1981, Australia was playing New Zealand in a one-day international cricket match. New Zealand batsman, Brian McKechnie, needed 6 runs off the last ball to win the game. Trevor Chappell's brother, Greg, the captain of the Australian team, ordered his brother to bowl the ball underarm (bowlers normally bowl overarm) and to roll the ball along the pitch.

At the time, the Chappell brothers' actions were legal under the laws of the game but considered rather unsportsmanlike but it did mean the action of bowling underarm was outlawed from the game.

The New Zealand Prime Minister, Robert Muldoon, referred to the incident as, 'the most disgusting incident I can recall in the history of cricket... it was an act of true cowardice and I consider it appropriate that the Australian team were wearing yellow.'

Harsh words.

But even our own Prime Minister, Malcolm Fraser, said the underarm ball was, 'contrary to the traditions of the game.'

We're over it, but the Kiwis, for some reason, still hold onto this one.

South Sydney Rugby League Club's 1909 Premiership

Fierce rivals, the two clubs agreed to boycott the Grand Final after the NSW Rugby League had announced plans to have a League v Union game. Unfortunately for Balmain, the South's team decided to turn up to play the game only to find they had no opposition and, therefore, won the title on a forfeit.

The 1971 Rugby Tour of South Africa (or any other of the Rebel tours)

Due to Apartheid, South Africa had been banned form international sporting competitions. When the Australians decided to tour South Africa in 1971 it sparked tremendous public outrage and protests against the system of racial inequality. There were later 'rebel' tours in sports such as cricket.

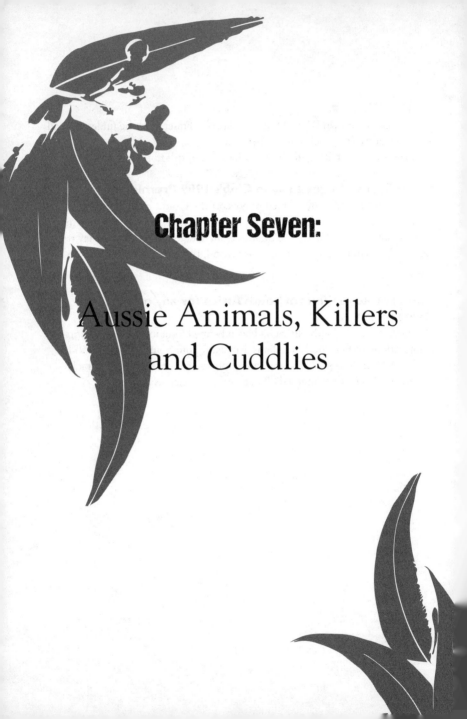

Chapter Seven:

Aussie Animals, Killers
and Cuddlies

The Cute Ones (Well, most of them are!)

The fact that Australia broke away from Pangaea at an early stage means that we have 90 percent of species that are only found in Australia. It also means that we have some of the most bizarre. Many Aussie animals, like the kangaroo and koala, will be familiar to the overseas traveller but there are many more cuties you might want to cuddle or killers you may want to avoid...

The Red Kangaroo (Macropus Rufus)

The most iconic of all Australian animals, our national airline, coat of arms etc. all carry this animal as its emblem. The red kangaroo is just one of the many species of kangaroo. A group of kangaroos is called a 'mob' and they can be found all over Australia. A Joey lives in its mother's pouch until it is ready to leave. Kangaroos, surprisingly for people from overseas, are sometimes considered a pest and culling is common. However, in many cases, if we do not cull them they will starve. Kangaroos can also be dangerous because, when threatened, males will balance themselves on their tails and kick out with their legs or begin boxing with their claws.

Fact: The Boxing Kangaroo is a national symbol.

Koala (Phascolarctos Cinereus)

An icon of Australia the koala is the cute creature that everyone from overseas wants to cuddle. Koalas eat only certain types of eucalyptus leaves and the low energy value of these leaves means koalas can sleep up to 20 hours a day. The word koala is, in fact, an Aboriginal word that means 'no drink' because they get their water from the eucalyptus leaves. However, don't be fooled. Koalas can be quite aggressive and have large claws.

Fact: Contrary to what is said in other countries, koalas are not bears!

Dingo (Canis Lupus Dingo)

The iconic Australian wild dog, the dingo came across with the Aboriginal people approximately 15000 years ago. Dingoes don't bark but they howl.

The dingo might seem like our everyday dog but they are best avoided, especially on places like Fraser Island, because they have been known to attack.

Fact: A dingo did eat her baby!

Honeypot Ant (Myrmecocystus)
A traditional bush tucker for people in Outback areas, honeypot ants have adapted to the harsh Australian climate by having certain ants whose job it is to store a sweet liquid for their mates to eat during the tough times.

The honeypot ant's abdomen will grow and grow and, when a worker ant becomes hungry they will go to their mate, and stroke his antenna. The honeypot ant senses this and begins to regurgitate the stored liquid.

Fact: Honeypot ants are eaten by Aboriginal people almost as a type of candy and are considered a bush tucker delicacy.

Platypus (Ornithorhynchus Anatinus)
A weird looking animal with the body of a beaver and the face of a duck the first Europeans to sight it thought it was God's joke. It is found in south-eastern Australia in freshwater rivers and creeks. They are nocturnal and use their webbed-feet to paddle around.

Fact: Male platypi are venomous with poisonous spines on their rear feet.

Emu (Dromaius Novaehollandiae)
Australia's largest bird is also flightless. Between 1.5 and 2 metres tall, the emu has three toes and runs very quickly on its large legs. The males look after the large green eggs. Emus are very common sights in the Outback and can sometimes be seen in suburban areas.

Fact: The emu is the world's second largest bird.

Cockatoo (Cacatuoidae)

There are several species of cockatoo, but the most well known member of the species is the sulphur-crested cockatoo. Named so because of the bright yellow crest on its head. Cockatoos are a very common sight in suburban areas and their loud screech often fills the afternoon sky. There is also another beautiful bird, the Gang-Gang cockatoo, or Black Cockatoo, whilst it is much rarer than its white-feathered cousin their numbers are beginning to increase.

Fact: Cockatoos, as pets, can often feel depressed if they don't get enough attention and affection from their owners.

Galah (Eolophus Roseicapilla)

Another member of the cockatoo family, the galah has pink and grey feathers with a white crest on its head. Galahs are very common and are found all across Australia.

Fact: Galahs, despite their clownish behaviour, mate for life.

Goanna (Varanus Varius)

A large member of the monitor family, the goanna can grow up to two metres in length. Goannas have various colours but they are mostly yellowish brown to blend in with their environment.

Fact: Some scientists have suggested that goannas can be somewhat venomous, particularly from the remaining bacteria in their mouths from the rotten carcasses they consume.

Frilled-Necked Lizard (Chlamydosaurus Kingii)

An iconic lizard that once appeared on the now discontinued two-cent coin, the Frilled-Neck Lizard is named so because of the large frill around its neck which, when angered or frightened, will flair.

Fact: A Frilled-Necked Lizard can run standing up on its hind legs.

Tasmanian Devil (Sarcophilus Harrisii)

Made famous by the Looney Tunes cartoon, Tasmanian Devils do not spin wildly in circles! They are, in fact, a small, dog-sized marsupial with black fur and sharp teeth. The Tassie Devil, as it is affectionately termed, is carnivorous and its name comes from the growling sounds it makes and the red reflection of its eyes, its appearance led the early settlers to believe there were devils in the forest.

Fact: A 10-kilogram Tassie Devil has the same bite force as a dog four times that size.

Echidna (Echidna Hystrix/ Tachyglossidae)

The Echidna's diet is mostly ants and, of course, it has spines on its back. When threatened the Echidna will roll into a ball and defend itself with its spines. As such, Echidnas are also known as spiny anteaters. The Echidna, along with the platypus, is one of two egg-laying mammals.

Fact: Echidnas are actually extremely good swimmers.

Tasmanian Tiger (Thylacinus Cynocephalus)

Also known as the Thylacine, this is one of the most intriguing and mysterious of Australian animals. It is in fact a large marsupial but given its name 'tiger' due to the striped patterns on its back. Endemic to the island of Tasmania the Tassie Tiger's fate was sealed with European settlement and the introduction of livestock. Bounties were placed on the tigers because they were attacking sheep and they were, literally, hunted to the point of extinction. Stories of the tiger still exist but there has yet to be any definitive proof to confirm this.

Fact: The last known tiger died in the early twentieth century.

Magpies (cracticus tibicen)

There are numerous types of magpies in Australia but, basically, they are from the shrike family and are generally back and white in colour. Magpies are very common in Australia and are often visitors in people's gardens. Magpies are generally friendly and have a lovely song but beware of them in spring.

Fact: Magpies can be very aggressive during nesting season and will swoop people running by or riding by on a bicycle.

Kookaburra (Dacelo Gigas)
A member of the Kingfisher family the Kookaburra is the largest bird of the family. Kookaburras are found across the country and are famed for their call that mimics a laugh. They mostly live on lizards and snakes but they have been known to steal food from people's BBQs.

Fact: An iconic Australia song is *Kookaburra Sits in the Old Gum Tree*. The famous Australia song, *Down Under*, was considered to be using parts of the original song and the band, Men At Work, were ordered to pay royalties accordingly.

Australia's Dangerous Animals: Killers on Land

Fierce Snake (Oxyuranus Microlepidotus)
Also called the Inland Taipan this snake looks, as its alternative name suggests, 'fierce'. With a deep black/ brown body this snake is the most venomous in the world. Needless to say, you don't want to be bitten by this guy. On the plus side, they live in the Outback and are more likely to hurry away than try to bite you.

Fact: One drop of Fierce Snake venom has the ability to kill 250, 000 mice.

Coastal Taipan (Oxyuranus Scutellatus)
A large and aggressive snake that lives in northern Australia, this snake is not to be approached! They can grow to more than two metres in length and, unlike other snakes that will flee if threatened, the Coastal Taipan is just as likely to strike again and again. They have highly potent venom making them the world's second most venomous snakes.

Fact: The Coastal Taipan's fangs are 12 millimetres long!

Eastern Brown Snake (Demansia Textilis)
The third most venomous snake in the world, the Eastern Brown is one of the most dangerous snakes in the country. Yes, its venomous, but the fact that the eastern brown lives in the most populated areas of Australia and can be found hanging around Australian homes looking for mice and rats means it often comes into contact with humans.

Fact: Snakes hear through vibrations and will generally disappear when they sense your vibrations. If you find you are confronted with a snake the best bet is to leave them alone and find a way out. Snakes will only attack if they feel threatened.

King Brown Snake (Pseudechis Australis)
As its name suggests, this is a very, very large snake. Found mostly in the northern parts of Australia it is also known as the Mulga snake, its colour varies depending on the climate in which it lives. Highly venomous and best left alone.

Fact: King Browns will bite again and again.

Death Adder (Acanthophis Antarcticus)
The most venomous Australian adder, the Death Adder is, as its name sounds: deadly.

A brownish yellow snake that hides in the undergrowth, the Death Adder will wait for days and days for its prey. Its tail appears like a small worm, which it wiggles to attract lizards and other animals, as the animal goes for the 'worm' the snake then makes its move on the prey.

Fact: Death Adders perfectly camouflage themselves in the leaf litter. If you are going bushwalking make sure you wear solid shoes and long trousers.

Tiger Snake (Notechis Scutatus)

A very common snake throughout south-eastern Australia and Tasmania, the Tiger Snake is named so because of the yellow-orange bands on its otherwise black body.

Fact: Snakes in South Australia are a protected species; killing one can incur fines upwards of $7500.

The Red-Bellied Black Snake (Pseudechis Porphyriacus)

One of the most common snakes you are likely to encounter, the red-bellied black, is named for its black body and red underside. Red-Bellies tend to live near water and in wetland areas. The Red-Belly is not actually extremely dangerous to people but if bitten hospital treatment must be sought.

Fact: Red-Belly poison is actually more poisonous to other snakes rather than humans as their venom is more potent to their favourite meal, other reptiles.

Funnel Web Spider (Atracinae- Atrax Robustus)

A nasty little critter, the funnel-web spider is a dark black spider measuring around 5cm in length. Funnel-webs are Australia's deadliest spider and, prior to modern medical advancements and anti-venoms, it was responsible for many deaths per year. Funnel-webs, as their name suggests, like to live in funnel-shaped webs, usually in dark, damp, moist places. Generally this is something like a log, but they have been known to make their burrows in people's boots and shoes. Any Aussie will tell you that, if you have left your shoes outside, it is always a good idea to check inside them first!

Fact: There have only been 13 recorded deaths from funnel-web bites.

Redback Spider (Latrodectus Hasselti)

One of the most famous Australian spiders, they are very small, (around 1 centimetre in length) and characterised by their black bodies and large red spot on their abdomen. Redbacks have cluttered and clumsy webs and they prefer to live in cool, damp, dark areas. This means they are very common around the house and in garden sheds. They have even been found in the dunny! Leading to there being a song by Slim Newton *Redback on the Toilet Seat*. Redback spiders are venomous.

Fact: Their venom is certainly life threatening to a small child but for an adult their bite is likely to make you very sick.

Cassowary (Casuarius Casuarius)
A large bird that lives in mostly north Queensland, the Cassowary has black feathers with a blue head and a red crest. Remnants of the dinosaur age, these birds are becoming more of a problem because people are feeding them and they are venturing into human habitats. However, don't feed them because, if agitated, they will lash out with the large claws on their feet.

Fact: The Cassowary is the second heaviest bird in the world, after the ostrich.

Local Knowledge: First Aid for Snakebite
Snakebites, contrary to what most overseas visitors believe, are generally not fatal, if treated correctly.

If bitten:

- Stay calm. The more stressed you are the more blood, therefore venom, rushes through your body.
- Apply an immobilisation bandage/ pressure bandage. This slows the spread of the venom but do not apply a tourniquet because you don't want to cut the blood off entirely.
- Put the bitten limb (and it is usually arms and legs, toes and fingers that are bitten) in an immobilisation bandage.
- Do not cut.
- Do not suck.

Australia's Dangerous Animals: Killers in the Water

Box Jellyfish (Carybdea Alata)
Box Jellyfish are named so because of the box-like shape of the upper-part of the jellyfish's body. These animals are deadly because their tentacles, which can reach metres in length, carry severely venomous poison. You might get stung without even seeing the animal.

Fact: If stung you have to neutralise the poison. As disgusting as this sounds human urine has this effect so you may need to pee on your mate, however, vinegar will do the same job. Found in the northern waters of Australia, a word of advice, do not swim in Australia's north.

Blue-Ringed Octopus (Hapalochlaena)
This interesting little character looks beautiful with its bright blue rings, but don't be fooled. It will kill you. Found in rock pools along the eastern shoreline of Australia, the blue-ringed octopus could fit in your hand but when you see the bright blue rings, beware! The parrot-like beak of the octopus will give you a nasty nip that will result in you being completely awake but your body completely paralysed as you die.

Fact: Blue-ringed octopus males will actually try to mate with one another.

Irukandji (Carukia Barnesi)
This tiny jellyfish lives in the northern waters of Australia. Despite its tiny size, 2.5cm, the Irukandji is a responsible for many summer deaths in Australia. Without treatment this tiny predator could kill you within days. A very, very tiny version of the Box Jellyfish this, only recently discovered jellyfish is even more venomous than its big cousin.

Fact: In order to discover the effects of an Irukandji sting, in 1961, a Dr Barnes stung himself and his son.

Cone Snail (Conus Marmoreus Linnaeus)

The Cone Snail is one of Australia's most deadly animals. Cone snails shoot a venomous harpoon to catch their prey and, if handled, they will inject that harpoon into humans. The larger cone snails are the most dangerous.

Fact: Cone snail venom has shown promising results in treating many human diseases.

Blue Bottles (Physalia Utriculus)

Locally known as 'Blue Bottles', this is the most common jellyfish that people are likely to come across. Their bodies can be up to 15 centimetres long and their tentacles can reach up to 10 metres. Many swimmers and surfers often get stung but the good news is, apart from a painful sting, the Blue Bottle is not considered deadly.

Fact: Thousands of people are stung by Blue Bottles each year.

Saltwater Crocodiles (Crocodylus Porosus)

These massive beasts are prehistoric relics that inhabit the northern waters of Australia. Crocodiles will have a go at just about anything. Crocodiles are actually a protected species. The ferocity and deadly predatory behaviour of these animals means if you see a sign in northern Australia that says don't swim, then, don't swim!

Fact: Saltwater crocodiles can grow up to 7 metres in length.

Great White Shark (Carcharodon Carcharias)

The most feared Australian animal and, probably one of the most dangerous; the Great White Shark is the iconic Australian predator. Great Whites can grow up to 5 metres long and weigh more than a ton. Great White Sharks don't deliberately attack people. They attack from below and often mistake body-boarders and surfers for turtles and seals. Their attacks are a test to see what someone is and they rarely attack a second time.

Fact: Great whites have 300 teeth in several rows. They can also replace their teeth.

Bull Shark (Carcharhinus Leucas)
While most people know the great white shark, the bull shark is responsible for more attacks on people. Bull sharks can survive in both fresh and salt water, which brings them more into contact with humans than other sharks. Bull sharks, as their name suggests, have very 'bullish' behaviour and this aggressive behaviour means they will go for just about anything.

Fact: Bull sharks are responsible for the most attacks on humans each year.

Tiger Shark (Galeocerdo Cuvier)
Known as the 'garbage cans of the ocean', tiger sharks will eat just about anything from license plates, fur coats to children's toys. Known to grow up to 5 metres in length, the tiger shark gets its name from the dark stripes down the sides of its body. While attacks from tiger sharks are rare, their size and teeth means bites from this shark are quite often fatal.

Fact: Whilst Australians are highly fearful of shark attacks the chances of actually being attacked by a shark are slim. Since the arrival of Europeans there have been 976 shark attacks with 232 of those fatal. When you do the sums that is less than one fatal attack per year.
      Your odds of being attacked by a shark are approximately 4 million to 1 – you have more chance of being struck by lightning!

Feral Animals and Invasive Species

Cane Toad (Bufo Marinus)
Introduced in 1935 to control the cane beetle, the cane toad is now a major pest in northern Australia. Difficult to exterminate, the cane toad has two venomous sacks on its back that secrete white venom, meaning it has no predators.

Fact: There are around 2 billion cane toads in Australia.

European Rabbit (Oryctolagus Cuniculus)
Rabbits were introduced into Australia in 1858 for recreational hunting purposes and as the saying goes, they have bred like rabbits. Rabbits have reached plague proportions and diseases such as Myxomatosis and Calicivirus has been employed to deal with their numbers.

Fact: In Western Australia there are actually three rabbit-proof fences, which measure 3256 kilometres (2023 miles).

Camel (Camelus Dromedarius)
Introduced in the 1840s, camels were brought to Australia to make exploration of the harsh interior more feasible. Due to their exceptional abilities to survive, the camel not only survived in the Aussie desert but also thrived. Camels cause great damage with their hooves, which damage the fragile desert vegetation and Aboriginal rock art. They can also foul or drain water sources. Camels have reached record numbers and there is an ongoing debate about how to control them.

Fact: There are approximately 1 million feral camels in Australia but culling and drought have reduced their numbers.

Feral Cat (Felis Catus)
Cats were first brought to Australia in 1849 as pets but with few predators, except for the dingo, cats thrived. People's domestic cats still cause problems in modern Australia and owners are encouraged to keep their cats inside or to have their cat wear bell collars to reduce the impact they have on small native mammals and birds.

However, many cats escape and become 'feral'. Growing much bigger than the normal domestic cat and much more aggressive, the feral cat is the most populous of introduced species and some scientists have suggested that these cats have been responsible for many extinctions of native animals.

Fact: Estimates put the number of feral cats as high as 20 million and, estimates also put the number of deaths from feral cats at many times their number.

Other Feral Animals
Australia also has water buffalo as well as feral horses, pigs, deer, dogs and donkeys.

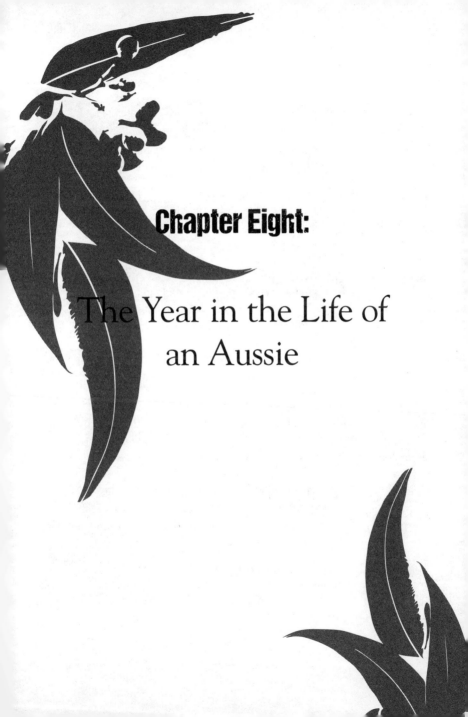

Chapter Eight:

The Year in the Life of an Aussie

Month	To See Who Aussies Are	Plan A: The Key Event	Plan B: The Alternatives
January	All about sun, surf, sand. Anything beach or fishing.	Australia Day	International cricket or the Australian Open tennis
February	A celebration of diversity.	Sydney Gay and Lesbian Mardi Gras	Clipsal 500 Melbourne Food and Wine Festival
March	To see how we party, and party fast.	Moomba	The F1 Grand Prix
April	What made us a country and gives us our identity.	ANZAC Day	The Sydney Royal Easter Show
May	Lovers of amazing spectacles!	Vivid Light Show	State of Origin
June	To see our strange and wild side!	Sydney Film Festival	Blue Mountains Winter Magic Festival
July	To see how seriously we don't take ourselves!	Darwin Beer Can Regatta	The Camel Cup
August	Having fun while we keep fit.	Sun-Herald City to Surf	Henley-on-Todd Regatta
September	National passions.	Rugby League and AFL Finals	Floriade
October	Two ends of the Aussie cultural spectrum.	The Bathurst 1000	Sculptures By The Sea
November	The best of Aussie sport (and how we love to have a bet!)	The Melbourne Cup	Australian Masters Golf
December	Fun in the sun with family and friends.	Christmas Day	Boxing Day Test/ Sydney to Hobart Yacht Race

January

Australia Day, 26 January

Australians celebrate their national day – Australia Day – with fun in the sun. It is a designated public holiday with hundreds of small and large events taking place across the nation. In Sydney, thousands of people gather along Sydney Harbour foreshore for the celebrations on the water. In towns and cities there are community breakfasts, beach parties, corroborees and concerts, parades and pageants, sporting events, cultural and historic exhibitions and fireworks displays. Citizenship ceremonies are held to welcome new residents and the best Aussies are honoured for their achievements. It's a day for Australians to celebrate everything that's great about being Australian. There's no better time to visit to meet Australians and see the country at its most relaxed.

www.australiaday.org.au

The Australian Open

The Australian Open is the Asia-Pacific Grand Slam and, as such, attracts all of the top tennis players from around the world. The Australian slam is a relaxed affair and it brings a uniquely Aussie perspective to a world sport but don't be fooled by the Open's nickname as the 'happy' slam. It is the first major tournament of the year and the competition is just as hot at the court temperatures.

www.ausopen.com

The Cricket

Summer in Australia means cricket. Each year different cricketing nations come to Australia. The Sydney Test Match begins on the 2nd of January but throughout January you also have the one-day internationals, international T20 games and the Big Bash League.

www.cricketaustralia.com

Summernats

A celebration of all things cars, particularly hotted-up streetcars. Staged at the Canberra Exhibition Park, competitions include the world's best burnout and precision driving displays. If rev-heads and the smell of rubber aren't your go there is always some of the most famous Aussie bands playing there to make the nights just as intense as the days.

www.summernats.com.au

Brisbane/ Sydney International Tennis

Two of the major warm-up tournaments for the Australian Open, the Brisbane International and the Apia Sydney International always have the highest quality tennis stars prepping and perfecting their game in readiness for the slam later in the summer.

www.brisbaneinternational.com.au
www.apiainternational.com.au

Sydney Festival

The Sydney Festival is the time of year when Sydney really comes alive. The festival aims to showcase all of Australia's talent from the arts to music. Concerts are held in the premier music venue, The Domain, in the centre of Hyde Park as well as circus and cabaret performances.

www.sydneyfestival.org

Santos Tour Down Under

This is Australia's version of the Tour de France. A carnival atmosphere surrounds this event and it is not only a chance to see some of the world's best professional riders but also the wonderful variety of landscapes of South Australia (and it provides the chance to try some of Australia's best wines from the Barossa Valley).

www.tourdownunder.com.au

February

Sydney Gay and Lesbian Mardi Gras

One of the biggest Gay and Lesbian events in the world, hundreds of thousands of people line the streets of Sydney to see the floats that cover scores of cultural, sporting and social themes. The Sydney Mardi Gras is a sensational display of colour, costumes, designs and dancing.

www.mardigras.org

Perth International Arts Festival

The Perth Arts Festival is the oldest annual festival in the southern hemisphere. The Festival showcases the best in theatre, music and film as well as many other community events. The festival has hundreds of events and reaches almost half a million people.

www.perthfestival.com.au

Clipsal 500

The national racing sport of Australia is V8 racing. It is called a V8 because the engines have four cylinders on each side in the shape of a V. The cars fly around the streets of Adelaide, reaching speeds of more than 300 kph. Along with the high-octane racing there are huge parties and concerts throughout the night.

www.clipsal500.com.au

Melbourne Food and Wine Festival

Melbourne, as a city, has fantastic wine bars and restaurants, many hidden amongst the alleys and laneways of the city. The festival also spreads out from the capital to encompass the beautiful wineries and landscapes of regional Victoria.

www.melbournefoodandwine.com.au

March

Moomba

Moomba is when Melbourne really comes alive. Held over the Victorian Labour Day Weekend, Moomba entails music, dance, sport, and fireworks across all of the city's streets and parks. Moomba culminates in the dazzling Moomba street parade and the wacky Birdman Rally where a whole bunch of crazy people dress up like birds and jump off a perfectly good platform.

www.moomba.com.au

Formula 1 Australian Grand Prix, Albert Park, Melbourne

The first grand prix of the season, the Australian Grand Prix always throws up some surprises as the F1 cars race around the streets of Melbourne. Being the first race of the season all the top teams are desperate to win this one and set themselves up for the season.

www.grandprix.com.au

April

Sydney Royal Easter Show

The Easter Show originated as a chance for the people from the country to come to the city and showcase and sell their cattle and livestock and produce. It has grown to be one of Australia's biggest annual events, attracting almost a million visitors each year. From agricultural and animal displays to the famed wood chopping competition, the Easter Show provides the foreign visitor with a chance to see everything that makes up rural Australia in one place.

www.eastershow.com.au

Byron Bay Blues Fest

Held near Tyagarah Tea Tree Farm, near Byron Bay in northern NSW, the Blues Fest can boast some of the biggest names in Blues and Roots, including the like of Paul Simon and Elvis Costello. Seven stages are surrounded by camping grounds in one of the most beautiful beachside areas of Australia.

www.bluesfest.com.au

Rip Curl Pro

Held at one of the most iconic beaches in Australia, Bell's Beach, this is one of the events on the ASP World Championship Tour that all the professional male and female surfers want to win. Bell's usually serves up huge waves and serves up even bigger parties.

www.ripcurl.com.au

ANZAC Day

ANZAC Day, the 25th of April, rivals Australia Day as Australia's biggest national celebration. ANZAC Day is the day we celebrate all of the soldiers that have served and died for our country. The day begins with people paying their respects at various dawn services around the country, with the biggest of these being at the Australian War Memorial. The remainder of the day involves a lot of drinking, pausing at 11am for the Last Post, and then spending the rest of the day playing Two-Up.

Local Knowledge: Two Up

One of the biggest traditions on ANZAC Day is the playing of Two-Up.

The game is played because, back in the First World War, the Australian soldiers in the trenches had a lot of spare time and, given that the Australian soldiers were the best paid in the world; they had a lot of money to spend. Australians love a bet so what did the Australian soldiers do with their time… they played Two-Up.

Two-Up involves placing three coins on a long wooden stick, ruler or something similar. The person who throws the coins in the air is called the 'spinner'. So, on Anzac Day you will hear the phrase, 'come in spinner'. Basically, what happens is that people in the crowd will bet with someone nearby about whether they think the coins will land with two or more heads or two or more tails. For example, a punter may call a bet of $20 on heads. Another punter will call the same amount but on tails. The spinner then steps into the middle of the circle and flips the coins. Depending on the outcome, one of the two punters will then double their money.

'All good,' I hear you say. 'An easy way to make money,' I hear you say.

However, this continues *all* day. People are known to call, 'One thousand he heads them!' It is easy to win big, but it is equally as easy to lose big too, hence why it is only legal to play Two-Up on ANZAC Day.

May

Aussie Wine Month
In recent decades the Australian wine industry, and Australian wines themselves, have gained an outstanding international reputation. Aussie Wine Month incorporates more than 100 events across the country and allows the foreign visitor to try the best of Australian Chardonnays, Cabernets, Sémillons and Shirazs in the famous wine regions of our country such as the Barossa and Hunter Valleys.

www.aussiewinemonth.com

Vivid Sydney
Vivid Sydney is a dazzling light festival, which involves some of the most creative minds composing a variety of light shows and projections on the Sydney Opera House and at other vantage points around the harbour. This is a highly popular event with families.

www.vividsydney.com

State of Origin Game 1

One of the fiercest inter-state rivalries, this is the first rugby league match between New South Wales and Queensland. For anyone that has never seen a rugby league match this is the best, and most brutal, rugby league you will ever see.

www.nrl.com.au

June

Sydney Film Festival

The Sydney Film Festival showcases some of the best cinema from both Australia and around the world. With over 250 screenings and films and documentaries the visitor to Australia not only gets to see great films but also to see them in some of the best theatres and open-air cinemas that Sydney has to offer.

www.sff.org.au

July

Super 15s Rugby Union final

Australian rugby union franchises, NSW Waratahs, Queensland Reds, ACT Brumbies, Western Force (Perth) and Melbourne Rebels, have had a mixed history in the Super 15s competition (formally Super 12s and 14s) over the past decades. Our Kiwi neighbours and South African rivals usually fight out the final, but it must be remembered the NSW Waratahs were crowned champions in 2014. The final is only played in Australia if one of the franchises finish top of the table … go the Tahs!

www.superxv.com

Darwin Lions Beer Can Regatta
If you wanted to escape the Australian winter and head to the warmth of the tropics one of the best events to see is the Darwin Beer Can Regatta. Held at Mindil Beach the aim of the regatta is to build your 'yacht' out of beer cans. The aim of the game: to stay afloat long enough to reach the finish line.

www.beercanregatta.com.au

Cairns Indigenous Arts Festival
A celebration of traditional Aboriginal and Torres Strait Islander art, music and dance. This is one of Australia's premier events with both Indigenous art sales and exhibitions. The Cairns Indigenous Arts Festival is a must to gain a greater understanding of the culture of the traditional owners of Australia.

www.ciaf.com.au

The Camel Cup
The Camel Cup is an exciting, if slightly strange, race that takes place in Alice Springs, in the Northern Territory, on the second Saturday of July. Camels can be crazy to ride, which makes for great entertainment for the spectators over the course of the nine races held. Belly dancing, rickshaw races, food stores, bars and kids' camel races make for one insane day out.

www.camelcup.com.au

August

Sun-Herald City to Surf
The most famous fun run in Australia, the City to Surf begins at Hyde Park in the centre of Sydney and winds its way over 14 kilometres until the finish line at the iconic Bondi Beach. Walkers to elite athletes make up the more than 85000 competitors. Whether you want to run or simply take in the

atmosphere the City to Surf is one of the best ways to take in the sights of Sydney.

www.city2surf.com.au

The Henley-on-Todd Regatta
(also called the Todd River Race)
The Todd River Regatta is a 'boat' race but not in the traditional sense of the word. The regatta is actually held in the usually dry Todd River in Alice Springs. People make metal boats or transform trucks into boats. Everybody dresses up with themes such as pirates and Vikings. Interestingly enough, the regatta had to be cancelled in 1993 when it rained.

www.henleyontodd.com.au

September

Floriade
This is when the nation's capital bursts into colour, with over a million flowers in bloom in a variety of displays that highlight Aussie inventions, celebrities, sports as well as other parts of our lifestyle and culture. Nightfest is one of the major events of Floriade with the colourful displays lit up by an array of light shows, accompanied by musical performances.

www.floriadeaustralia.com.au

October

The Rugby League and AFL Grand Finals
September is finals season and October is the time for the grand finals, where the best teams from both rugby league and Australian Rules Football face off.

With each grand final for each code attracting upwards of 100000 people, get yourself a beer, a pie, a hot dog, and take in a truly unique Aussie experience.

www.afl.com.au
www.nrl.com.au

Sculpture by the Sea
A mix of 100 serious, fun and crazy sculptures out in the open air along one of the greatest coastal walks in Australia. Stretching from Bondi Beach and along the rocky coastline to Tamarama, the visitor not only experiences the best of Australian art but also the art of Australian nature.

www.sculpturebythesea.com

Bathurst 1000
Bathurst, one of the oldest inland cities in Australia and a three-hour drive from Sydney, holds one of the most iconic of Australian motor races, the Bathurst 1000 around Mount Panorama. As the name suggests is a one thousand lap, endurance race for V8 cars. V8 racing is not only fast-paced but is extremely close and cars have been forced to retire after they have hit a kangaroo. This is one of the biggest weekends for petrol heads and race-lovers alike, definitely worth a visit.

www.v8supercars.com.au

November

Melbourne Cup Spring Racing Carnival
The 'race that stops the nation' has been run for more than 150 years and attracts the best horses from around the globe as they attempt to claim the famous gold cup. The Melbourne Cup Carnival is not just about the racing.

It is also about the fashion as the ladies wear all of the latest styles and bring out their fascinators while the boys dress up in their best suits.

www.melbournecup.com.au

Australian Masters Golf
Australia has not only increased the number of internationally ranked golfers from our fair shores but also has a reputation for building and designing some of the most beautiful, yet toughest, golf courses. The Masters was traditionally played at Huntingdale Golf Club but it is now played on a rotating basis. Watch as the world's best golfers compete for the coveted gold jacket.

www.australianmasters.com.au

Margaret River Gourmet Escape
Margaret River is one of the world's best surfing locations but it is also famed for its quality wines and food. The Gourmet Escape brings together some of the best chefs, food and produce. Taken together with a festival atmosphere and beautiful landscapes the Escape is one of Western Australia's premier events.

www.gourmetescape.com.au

December

Tropfest Australia
Tropfest began as a short-film festival for just family and friends in a small café in 1993. Over the last two decades it has grown to become one of the biggest stages for filmmakers to gain international exposure. The best of the best films are showcased around the country but the finalist's film is shown at Sydney's Centennial Park.

www.tropfest.com.au

The Sydney to Hobart Yacht Race

One of the world's toughest yacht races, the Sydney to Hobart race takes place on Boxing Day every year. It begins in Sydney Harbour and finishes at Hobart's Constitution Dock. First contested in 1945, the race covers a distance of 630 nautical miles (1170 kilometres). The fastest yachts complete the race in around 2 days and, depending on the weather conditions for year to year, even the biggest boats can get into trouble. *Wild Oats XI* currently holds the record for the fastest completion of the race and for the most number of race wins.

www.rolexsydneyhobart.com

Chapter Nine:

Made in Australia - 25 Aussie Ideas that Changed the World

The Refrigerator/ Ice Making Machine
An invention that literally changed the way we live, it can be found in just about every household in the world. In 1856, James Harrison, a journalist who emigrated from Britain, developed the first practical vapour compression refrigeration system and he released his first commercial ice-making machine in 1854.

The Underwater Torpedo
A weapon that revolutionised naval warfare, it was created by Louis Brennan, an Irish-born Australian, in 1877. It was propelled by two rotors that were spun by quickly pulling attached wires from a drum inside the torpedo. Other guided torpedoes had been developed before, but this was the first one that worked at the correct distance and speed.

The Notepad
As long as paper had existed it had been either kept in loose sheets or bound together in a long and expensive process. In 1902, the stationer, Birchall's of Launceston in Tasmania, decided it would be a good idea to cut the size of the paper in half, whack some cardboard on the back and glue everything at the top. Pure genius.

Feature Film – the Story of the Kelly Gang
In 1906 Australia produced, according to the UNESCO Memory of the World Register, the first full-length feature film. Written by Charles Tait and starring Elizabeth and John Tait, the film cost £400 to make and grossed £25000 at the Box Office. The film runs for more than an hour and was first shown in country towns. Due to its popularity it had already covered its production costs by the time it was shown at the Athenaeum Hall in Melbourne on Boxing Day, 1906. The film was banned twice in 1907 and 1912 because Victorian authorities objected to the glorification of criminals. The film screened for more than twenty years and was shown as far away as New Zealand and the British Isles.

The Tank

Lancelot Eldin 'Lance' de Mole was a South Australian engineer and inventor who, in an amazing feat of foresight, went to the British Authorities in 1912 (and again in 1914 and 1916) with preliminary designs for the world's first tank. De Mole's submission were lost in the bureaucracy and it was not until 1919, after the development of other tanks, that de Mole was given the recognition he deserved. A Royal Commission later concluded that de Mole's designs were far better than what was used in the war and that, had his designs been used, the tank would have entered the war earlier. Who knows how different the war may have been!

Electronic Pacemaker

In 1926 two Australian doctors, Mark C. Lidwell and Edgar H. Booth, created the world's first pacemaker. It was a portable device that was constructed of two poles, one of which had a needle that was inserted into the cardiac chamber. Despite its crude nature, it did revive a stillborn child at a Sydney hospital in 1928.

Coupe Utility

Affectionately known in Australia as 'the Ute'. As opposed to other pick-ups the Ute was meant to be a roomier coupe-styled vehicle with a useable cargo tray. The Ute came about because of a 1932 letter from a Victorian farmer who wrote to Ford Australia and requested: 'a vehicle to go to Church in on a Sunday and which can carry our pigs to market on Mondays.' Ford obliged and, in 1934, after designer, Lew Bandt had developed it, the Ute was released and in the decades since the Ute has become an Aussie Legend.

Splayd

In the traditional Aussie way of making things simpler and shorter, William McArthur, designed the Splayd in the late 1940s– a mixture of a knife, spoon and fork. Developed in Sydney, the Splayd has spread to be used throughout the world and has sold over 5 million units since its release.

Hills Hoist

The Hills Hoist is a clothesline that is adjustable and spins. Others had similar ideas of such clothes drying devices but, Lance Hill, in South Australia in 1945, was pressured by his wife to find a more sophisticated and productive (and less expensive) manner of drying her clothes. The Hills' Hoist clotheslines became a cultural icon of Australia in the 1950s and 1960s and can be found dotted across most backyards in Australia today.

The Victa Lawnmower

The lawnmower has been around for a long time but in 1951, Mervyn Victor (trying to help his son's lawn mowing business) developed a new design in rotary lawn mowers.

Victor wanted to make a mower that was cheaper, lighter and more powerful. His first design was made out of scrap metal and a peach tin for a fuel tank – giving the first Victa lawnmower, the 'Peach-tin Prototype'. Victor's design has made the Sunday morning ritual so much easier for people the world over.

Stainless Steel Braces

To all the teenagers around the world who hate wearing braces, Australia says 'sorry' because we invented them. But, any modern teenager who complains needs to have a look at the methods used to straighten teeth before Percy Raymond Begg of Adelaide and, metallurgist, Arthur Wilcox, developed the world's first stainless steel braces in 1956.

The Black Box Flight Recorder

Even though the actual device is orange, this is an invention that is now in every plane in the world and has helped aviation authorities to understand much more about aircraft accidents. The black box has a flight data recorder (FDR) and the cockpit voice recorder (CVR) which, taken together, gives an accurate picture of what happened in a crash. Between 1953 and 1954 there was a series of accidents of De Havilland planes and Dr David Warren, who worked for the company, was assigned to discover the causes. Realising there were often no evidence or witnesses to a crash he developed the Black Box recorder in 1958.

Ultrasound

Most people in the world will have had an ultrasound procedure. Doctors in the 1950s were concerned about the negative effects of X-Rays on pregnant women. It works on oscillating, high pressure frequency sound waves and, while others around the world had attempted and experimented with this technology, Australians David Robinson and George Kossoff, developed Australia's first ultrasound scanner. By 1962 it was concluded that the Australian version was both technologically more proficient and more commercially viable.

Inflatable Escape Slide and Raft

Now a recognisable safety device on every plane the world over, the slide and raft were developed by Jack Grant, working for QANTAS (Queensland and Northern Territory Air Service), in 1965. Strangely enough, QANTAS is considered to be one of the safest airlines in the world.

The Plastic Wine or 'Goon' Cask

An absolute Aussie icon (and something that also doubles as a pillow and a floating device in the water) the plastic wine cask was developed by Thomas Angove, of Angove Wines in Renmark, South Australia in 1966. The plastic wine cask is made of polyethylene and prevents air from reaching the wine, thus making it last much, much longer.

Electronic Powerboard

A device that has allowed households the world over to use multiple devices at once (especially important in the days of TV/DVD/ PlayStation and X-Box) the Powerboard (multiple power points in one board) was developed by Peter Talbot working for Kambrook in 1972.

RaceCam

Watching motor racing today, or a myriad of other sports, would seem lost without RaceCam. In 1979, engineer, Geoff Healey, working for Australia's Channel 7 Network dreamt up the idea and incorporated it into their live racing broadcasts.

The Bionic Ear

An Aussie invention that dramatically changed the lives of hearing impaired people the world over. Born in Camden, NSW, Professor Graeme Clark was the pioneer of this technology. Clarks' thinking was that if one could bypass the damaged or underdeveloped section of the ear and electrically stimulate the auditory nerve then sound could be simulated. Clark's breakthrough moment came on a visit to the beach when he thought about using a seashell to reproduce the human cochlear. His vision was correct and thus, in 1979, was born the Cochlear Implant or Bionic Ear.

Dual Flush Toilet

Australia is the driest continent on earth and, as such, we often have water restrictions placed upon us. Prior to 1980, Aussies only had the full flush dunny, which, of course, wasted valuable water. Bruce Thompson, working for Caroma, developed to dual toilet (full and half flush), which is credited with saving more than 32000 litres of water for each household in Australia per year.

The Baby Safety Capsule

In Australia, and hopefully in other nations, having a child restrained whilst in the car is a no brainer but, even in Australia, this was not always the case. Compulsory seat belt laws were enacted in Australia in the 1960s and 1970s but car seat belts were found to be ineffective in the prevention of injury and death to children. In response to this, Bob Botell and Bob Heath, developed the 'Safe 'n Sound' Baby Safety Capsule in 1984. The capsule ingeniously slots into existing seat belts and are now compulsory across Australia.

Frozen Embryo Baby

While we didn't invent babies, or frozen embryo technology, the world's first embryo baby was born in Melbourne on the 28th of March 1984.

The Polymer Bank Note

Polymer bank notes are, of course, made of polymer and they have extra, added security features that paper banknotes don't possess. They also last longer than traditional paper notes. The Reserve Bank of Australia (RBA), the CSIRO (Commonwealth Scientific and Industrial Research Organisation) and the University of Melbourne developed these notes. The first notes were issued in 1988 (the same year as Australia's Bicentenary) and by 1996 Australia had completely changed to polymer notes. Polymer notes are now used in many countries around the world.

The Long-Wear Contact Lens

As part of an international research team, the CSIRO and the University of New South Wales strove to develop a more durable and easy-wear contact lens. They succeeded and, in 1991, they created a thin, long-lasting lens that has helped improve people's eyesight the world over.

Wi-Fi

An Aussie radio-astronomer, John O'Sullivan, discovered a key breakthrough in Wi-Fi technology except it was only because of, 'a failed experiment to detect exploding mini black holes the size of an atomic particle.' In 1992, the CSIRO gained patents for methods used to 'un-smear' the signal. Whilst the CSIRO developed this, other advancements in Wi-Fi were made elsewhere.

So, there is controversy about whether Aussies actually invented Wi-Fi, but we'll claim it anyway.

Spray-On Skin

Taking a small patch of a patient's healthy skin, growing more healthy skin in a laboratory and spraying that skin on a patient's damaged skin is a simple idea, but an ingenious one at that. Developed in 1999, by Professor Fiona Wood, spray-on skin helped treat victims of the Bali Bombings in 2002 and has been credited with saving almost 30 lives.

Chapter Ten:

The Aussie Index

An Aussie Collection of Curious Stats and Facts

85%	The number of Australians who live within 50km of the coast. Most of those on the eastern side.
$598	The amount Australia's richest woman, Gina Rinehart, earns every second.
23 million	The population of Australia and the clock is still ticking.
200	The number of Australians who wanted to break away and form a country in South America called 'New Australia'.
10	The number of sails on Sydney Opera House.
1250	The average number of UFO sightings in Australia each year.
3.4 billion	The age of the oldest fossil found in Australia.
70	The number of tourists who overstay their visa EVERYDAY! (And we worry about boat people!)
6 million	The number of Australians who watched Will and Kate's wedding.
300	The number of convict women who mooned the Governor of Tasmania in 1832.
20	The percentage of the world's poker machines in Australia.
2	Australia was the second country to give women the vote (behind the bloody Kiwis!).
11	The number of seconds it took for former Prime Minister, Bob Hawke, to consume 2.5 pints of beer.
31	The largest victory of an Australian soccer team (against Samoa in 2001).
5.18	Number of Aussies for every Kiwi.
1902	Prior to this date it was illegal to swim during the day (presumably to prevent shark attack – except sharks are more likely to attack at dusk and dawn!)
1	The length, in centimetres, of a baby kangaroo when it is born.

96	The average number of litres of beer an Aussie drinks each year.
63	The percentage of Australians that are overweight.
$29	The average amount each Australian bet on the 2014 Melbourne Cup.
162,000	The number of convicts sent to Australia from the United Kingdom throughout the period of transportation.
50.7°C	The highest ever recorded temperature in Australia. Reached at Oodnadatta airport in January 1960.
-23°C	The lowest ever recorded temperature in Australia. Reached at Charlotte's Pass in June 1994.
2.17	Approximate numbers of kangaroos per person.
5.5 million	The number of migrants (until 1996) who have settled in Australia since the end of the Second World War.
5614	The length, in kilometres, of the Dingo Fence that keep the dingoes to the north and the sheep and cattle safe to the south. It runs from Queensland to South Australia.
71.1	The average weight, in kilograms, of an Australian.
12.5	The average number of unprovoked shark attacks in Australia over the last decade.
146	The kilometre length of the longest straight road in Australia, on the Nullarbor Plain in Western Australia.
22	The percentage of Australians who can clearly claim convict ancestry.
200	The number of different world languages spoken in Australia and the number of countries where Australia has migrants.
17	The number of World Heritage sites Australia possesses.
500	The number of National Parks in Australia. Also the number of Australian soldiers who died in the Vietnam War.
80	The percentage of Australians who believe in aliens (only 74 per cent believe in the existence of God).

2 million	The number of Greeks living in Melbourne. (Melbourne is the largest 'Greek' city outside of Athens).
1979	The last time someone died from a spider bite in Australia.
15	The percentage increase of koalas dying from chlamydia.
400	The amount the town of Esperance, Western Australia fined NASA for littering when part of their Skylab satellite landed in their town.
23677	The size (in square kilometres) of Anna Creek, South Australia. The biggest cattle station in Australia. This is about the same size as Israel.
7, 692, 024	The number of square kilometres of Australia.
348	The height of Uluru in metres.
1.65	The average number of children for each Australian family.
5.9	The size in metres of the biggest Great White Shark caught in Australia.
126	The number of plant and animal species that have become extinct since European settlement.
7.2	The strongest earthquake recorded in Australia. It occurred in Meeberrie, Western Australia.
16	The number of times Queen Elizabeth II has visited Australia.
82.10	The average life expectancy of Australians.
6000	The number of species of flies in Australia.
919	The number of thongs washed up on Australian beaches each year.

The Aussie ABC: An Iconic Alphabet

A is for Australiana: a collective term used to refer to anything that is quintessentially, and possible kitsch, Australian. Boardies with the Australian flag on it, boxer shorts with the Australian flag on it, thongs with the Australian flag on it.

B is for Bring Back the Biff: Rugby league was famous in the past for big punch-ons. The modern game has attempted to outlaw this but there are many who would like to see a return to the 'biff', or fighting, of days gone by. 'Bring Back the Biff', was a movement created by former rugby league player, Mathew Johns, who created a bogan persona called Reg Reagan who sported a black shirt spouting the same phrase.

C is for Cork Hat: The two most annoying things in Australia: sunburn and flies. As such, Aussies created a solution to both ... the cork hat. The hat is a simple, wide-brimmed hat with strings hanging down from it with corks attached to the end of each string. As the wearer moved about the corks swing, keeping the flies away and the size of the hat keeps off the sun.

D is for Darwin Stubby: A stubby is a 375ml beer in most states of Australia. However, in the Top End they like to do things big and, because it gets so hot, they need a little more refreshment. A Darwin stubby is a 2.25 litre beer filled with NT Draught.

E is for Edmund Barton: Edmund Barton was the first Prime Minister of Australia from 1901 to 1903. He was a big player in the Federation movement, which pushed for Australian independence. Barton resigned from the position to become a judge in the High Court of Australia (which he also helped to establish). Barton died in 1920.

F is for Freemantle Doctor: The Freemantle Doctor is a Western Australian slang term for a cooling afternoon sea breeze that occurs during the summer. The Doctor comes in between midday and three in the afternoon and provides welcome relief from the summer heat. The name 'Freemantle' comes from the fact that the wind blows out of the south-west, from the direction of the coastal city of Freemantle.

G is for Ghan, The: The Ghan is a train journey that runs over the 2979 kilometres (1851 miles) between Adelaide and Darwin. The Ghan runs once a week in each direction and the trip itself takes three days and two nights. The train began its travels in 1929 and there are currently 14 stations along the line. The name 'Ghan' comes from the original 'Afghan' camel drivers who paved the way for Outback expansion.

H is for Home and Away: *Home and Away* is a long-running Australia TV Soap set in the fictional beach town of Summer Bay. Beginning in 1988, *Home and Away* is Australia's second longest running soap opera and it has gained international popularity (particularly in the United Kingdom) due to the beach lives of the characters. *Home and Away* remains one of Australia's most popular shows.

I is for Iron Ore: One of the main raw materials used in the production of steel. Iron ore is, arguably, the second most important commodity after oil. Australia, fortunately for us, has a lot of the stuff and iron ore has played its part in what Aussies refer to as the 'mining boom'.

J is for Jamberoo: Jamberoo is a small village near Kiama in New South Wales and it is also a name given to a popular, nearby action Water Park. The park originally started as a dairy, but soon proved unviable so the owners turned it into a grass skiing facility. It steadily grew from there into a water-based theme park and it has grown in popularity in the last twenty years, leading to the park expanding the range and excitement level of their rides.

K is for Kelpie: The kelpie is the classic Australia sheep dog. The kelpie is smart and loyal and can grow up to 20 kg and live between 10 and 15 years. The kelpie musters sheep and cattle with little or no guidance. There is evidence that the kelpie was crossbred with the dingo in the past but few people will admit to that due to the dingos' sheep killing tendencies.

L is for Lone Pine: Lone Pine is one of the most famous battles of the Gallipoli campaign. The battle occurred between the 6th and 10th of August, 1915.

Facing overwhelming enemy numbers the Australians managed to take the Turkish trenches and hold them. The name Lone Pine comes from the one pine tree left surviving at the completion of the battle.

M is for Marn Grook: Marn Grook is an Aboriginal word coming from the Gunditjmara language meaning 'game ball' but the term is generally used to a series of Aboriginal recreational pastimes and games. Marn Grook is believed to have connections with Australian Rules Football and the link between the two is demonstrated in the large number of Indigenous people playing AFL.

N is for Neighbours: Set on the fictional Ramsey Street in the fictional town of Erinsborough, *Neighbours* began in 1985 and is Australia's longest running television drama series. *Neighbours* has been a launching platform for a string of Australian success stories, particularly in the singing industry with Kylie Minogue, Delta Goodrem and Natalie Imbruglia beginning life as teens on the show. Guy Pearce also went on to become a successful Hollywood actor.

O is for Oodnadatta Track: The Oodnadatta Track is an unsealed Outback road stretching for 620km (385 miles).

P is for Patterson's Curse: Patterson's Curse is a pretty, purple-flowered plant, which is a highly invasive introduced plant. The plant is called Patterson's Curse because it is poisonous to livestock, particularly horses.

Q is for Quokka: The quokka is the symbol of Rottnest Island, off the coast of Perth, Western Australia. The quokka is a marsupial about the size of the domestic cat.

R is for Rats of Tobruk: The Rats of Tobruk is the name given to a group of Australian soldiers who fought in North Africa in 1941, against Erwin Rommel and the Afrika Korp. 14000 Australians, under severe conditions, held Tobruk, a key port in Libya. The name 'Rats' came from the fact that the Australians were dug in deep and often came out and collected up the remnants of battles to be used for their own purpose. Radio Berlin had referred to the men as 'rats caught in a trap'. The Aussies liked this and gave themselves the name.

S is for Swimming Pools: Australia has more domestic swimming pools, per capita, than anyone else in the world. There are an estimated 800,000 swimming pools in our country, meaning approximately 1 in 4 Australian homes have a pool and at, any given time, there is 40 million litres of water in Aussie pools.

T is for Tied Test Matches: There have only been two tied Test matches (out of 2000 games) in the history of cricket, one in 1960 and the other in 1986. Both games ended at the very end of the fifth day. Australia was involved in both ties, the 1960 game was against the West Indies and the 1986 game was against India.

U is for Ultraviolet: Australia is hot, damn hot, but the real killer is the UV rays. Australia has the highest rate of melanoma (skin cancer) in the world. According to the Australian Sun Council the average person will begin to burn after only 11 minutes in the sun during an average Aussie summer's day.

V is for Volkswagen: Yes, the Volkswagen is German, but the Kombi van has become an iconic Australian surf vehicle and, prior to modern SUVs and Motor Homes, the Kombi was the van of choice to travel around the country.

W is for Welcome Stranger: The Welcome Stranger is the biggest alluvial gold nugget ever found, weighing almost 72 kilograms (over 3000 ounces). It measured 61cm by 31cm and was found in Moliagul, Victoria in 1869. It is estimated that the nugget, in today's terms, would be worth almost $4 million.

X is for the Xantippe Mine: The Xantippe Mine is in the south west of Western Australia about 350 kilometres from Perth.

Y is for Yabba: Yabba (aka Stephen Harold Gascoigne) is an iconic Australian sports fan that was known as a serial heckler. Yabba would sit on the old hill at the Sydney Cricket Ground (with the grassed area of the grand being named after him until the redevelopments of the ground took the hill away). Some of Yabba's famous insults included: 'Send 'im down a piano and see if he can play that one.' And to an English batsman 'adjusting' himself, 'those are the only balls you've touched all day!'

Z is for Zinc Cream: the stuff Australian cricketers and other Australians put on their nose and face to block out the powerful Australian sun.

Local Knowledge: The Last You Need to Know About Aussies

The Australian National Anthem

Australia's national anthem, until 1973, was *God Save the Queen*, due to our British heritage. In the modern world Australia decided it needed an anthem of its own so a competition was held, attracting more than a thousand entries with prize money awarded.

The entries were substandard so the list was reduced to three songs, *Advance Australia Fair*, *Waltzing Matilda* and *Songs of Australia*. To make a choice the government asked 60000 people and *Advance Australia Fair* was, by a vote of more than half, the preferred choice.

Written by Peter Dodds McCormack in 1878, *Advance Australia Fair* originally had four verses but only two (the first and third) verses have been retained (although, to be honest, many Australians, until recently, probably still don't know the second verse!).

The abridged version (the one that is played during Olympic gold medal presentations) does include the last two lines of the third verse.

In 1978 a referendum was held to decide whether we wanted *Advance Australia Fair* or *Waltzing Matilda* and *Advance Australia Fair* won. The fact that *Waltzing Matilda* had too many colonial references and was the story of stealing a sheep, arguably went against it being adopted. *Waltzing Matilda* is the 'unofficial' national anthem, often sung at the climax of sporting events.

Australians are very proud of their nation, and its anthem, so it must be treated with respect at all times. It is customary to stand when it is played and to stand in a respectful fashion.

Advance Australia Fair

Australians all let us rejoice for we are young and free.
With golden soil and land for toil.
Our home is girt by sea. Our land abounds in nature's gifts of beauty, rich and rare.
In history's page, let every stage, Advance Australia Fair.

Beneath our radiant Southern Cross.
We'll toil with hearts and hands.
To make this Commonwealth of ours,
Renowned of all the lands.
For those who've come across the seas;
We've boundless plains to share.
With courage let us all combine,
To Advance Australia Fair.
In joyful strains then let us sing,
Advance Australia Fair.

Waltzing Matilda
(Australia's Unofficial National Anthem)

A few pieces of information and a few words of translation before you begin....

It is commonly thought that the billabong where this occurred is in Winton, Queensland.

Swagman: a traveller (mostly during the Depression) that roamed the country looking for work.
Coolabah: a type of eucalyptus tree.
Billabong: a small lake.
Billy: a tin can with a handle, boiled over a fire and used as a teapot.
Jumbuck: a sheep.
Matilda: a 'swag' or sleeping bag.
Tucker Bag: a bag for carrying food.
Squatter: rich landowners.

The Song

Once a jolly swagman camped by a billabong,
Under the shade of a Coolabah tree,
And he sang as he watched and waited till his billy boil,
You'll come a Waltzing Matilda with me.

Waltzing Matilda, Waltzing Matilda,
You'll come a Waltzing Matilda with me,
And he sang as he watched and waited till his billy boil,
You'll come a Waltzing Matilda with me.

Down came a jumbuck to drink at that billabong,
Up jumped the swagman and grabbed him with glee,
And he sang as he shoved that jumbuck in his tucker-bag,
You'll come a Waltzing Matilda with me.

Waltzing Matilda, Waltzing Matilda,
You'll come a Waltzing Matilda with me,
And he sang as he shoved that jumbuck in his tucker-bag,
You'll come a Waltzing Matilda with me.

Up rode the squatter mounted on his thoroughbred,
Down came the troopers one, two, three,
Who's that jolly jumbuck you've got in your tucker-bag?
You'll come a Waltzing Matilda with me.

Waltzing Matilda, Waltzing Matilda,
You'll come a Waltzing Matilda with me,
Who's that jolly jumbuck you've got in your tucker-bag?
You'll come a Waltzing Matilda with me.

Up jumped the swagman sprang in to the billabong,
'You'll never catch me alive!' said he,
And his ghost may be heard as you pass by that billabong,
You'll come a Waltzing Matilda with me.

Waltzing Matilda, Waltzing Matilda,
You'll come a Waltzing Matilda with me,
And his ghost may be heard as you pass by that billabong,
You'll come a Waltzing Matilda with me.

Resources and Essential Reading

Blake, B, & Smitz, P, **Australian Language and Culture**, Lonely Planet, Footscray, 2007.

Butler, S., **The Dinkum Dictionary: The Origins of Australian Words, 3rd Edition**, Text Publishing, Melbourne, 2009.

Clark, M., **A History of Australia**, Melbourne University Press, Melbourne, 1962.

Craven, I., **Australian Popular Culture**, Cambridge University Press, Sydney, 1994.

Foster, Jason K., **A Century of Anzacs**, New Holland Publishers, 2014.

Jupp, J., **The Australian People: An Encyclopaedia of the Nation, its People, and their Origins**, Cambridge University Press, Sydney, 2001.

Moore, B., **Speaking Our Language: The Story of Australian English**, Oxford University Press, Melbourne, 2008.

Pennery, B., **Australia: Culture Smart: The Essential Guide to Customs and Culture**, Kuperard, London, 2006.

Perry, M., Vallance, C., & Parish, S., **1000 Questions and Answers about Australia**, Steve Parish Publishing, Sydney, 2001.

Sharp, I., **Cultureshock! Australia: A Survival Guide to Customs and Etiquette**, Marshall Cavendish, Singapore, 2012.

Turner, G., **Making It National: Nationalism and Australian Popular Culture**, Allen & Unwin, St Leonard's, 1994.

www.immi.gov.au – the Department of Immigration and Citizenship has many booklets for advice on visiting or moving to Australia.

www.australia.com – the official tourism website of Australia contains many ideas on places to go, things to do and suggested itineraries.

www.australia.gov.au – contains quick summaries of everything Australian.

www.alldownunder.com – a quirky little website that contains facts about Australia from famous peoples' birthdays to Aussie Christmas songs.

www.australiatravelsearch.com.au – a wonderful site that acts as a search engine for anything to do with Aussie travel.

www.abs.gov.au – statistics on absolutely everything to do with Australia.

www.creativespirits.info – a great site that contains excellent information about Aboriginal Australians.

www.australian-animals.net – brief summaries of all our wonderful wildlife.

www.koalanet.com.au – a comprehensive site of Aussie slang terms and meanings.

www.australiancultureandcustoms.com – details the dos and don'ts about how to act in Australia and has some good links to more detailed sites about Aussie culture.

Index